Holy Smoke! It's Mezcal!

Holy Smoke! It's Mezcal!

A COMPLETE GUIDE FROM AGAVE TO ZAPOTEC

JOHN McEVOY

Mezcal PhD Publishing

First Edition

Designed by Patty Fabricant
Library of Congress Cataloging-In-Publication Data
McEvoy, John 1964-
Holy Smoke! It's Mezcal! The Complete Guide from Agave to Zapotec / by John McEvoy

ISBN 978-0-9903281-0-0 : Softcover

Contents

DISTILERIA
PORFIDIO
S.A.
JALISCO
MEXICO
SINGLE-BARREL
SPIRIT OF MEXICO

Foreword

Dear Tequila,

I want you to know how truly special you are to me, and the tremendous amount you've meant to me over our wonderful years together. You've been there on the best days of my life, and brought me through some of the more difficult times as well. You need to know that it's not you. It's me.

I know we've had some amazing times together, and our memories are special and I will always cherish them. How about Cozumel in the mid-'90s? I discovered how magical you were in that gorgeous bottle of Porfidio. You were sweet, earthy, full-bodied and bursting with life. I think that was the day when I realized you were not just a flirtatious fling, but someone whom I could be with forever.

Remember Napa? Yes I was tempted by all those young, precocious wines, but it was you in the back of the limo, not them. Our relationship flourished, and you got your own shelf, which soon became a cabinet, and then finally a closet! You fulfilled me with your richness, smooth caramels and luscious vanillas. I was so intoxicated by your presence.

Please know I was never tempted to stray. Sure I tried the occasional Cosmo, but really, I never wavered. Appletinis caused many to wander (and lose their manhood), but I stayed the course. I introduced you to my important clients, my friends, my family. They all loved you, especially my mom.

We rolled into the mid-2000s and I began to envision us retiring to the beach someday. You seduced me with your barrel aging and extra anejos: Don Julio 1942, Herradura Suprema and Chinaco Negro, to name a few. And finally, just when I thought it couldn't get any better, there was the Asombroso 11-year Anejo. You were sublime ... like honey. I was self-actualized. You made me a happy man.

But my dearest Tequila, something has changed in recent years. I still care for you and I love you, but I am no longer in love with you. And even worse,

I must admit there is someone else. I am so ashamed, as it is someone you know. A relative of yours. She is born of the same family, has the same bloodlines, and has lived much of the storied life that you have, yet she is different.

Her differences are at times subtle, but more frequently, pronounced. She is smoky, sexy and complex. She comes from the earth, from Mayahuel, and was perhaps here before colonial times. She has lived through famine, drought, wars and banishment. She has been illegal and looked down upon, but still, she held her head high. Her name? Mezcal.

And now my love, her time has arrived. I did not find her, yet somehow she found me. At first it was casual, but admittedly I found myself returning to her sultry ways. While you were my first love, she beguiles me with her character and depth, and yes, I was with her on those nights when you could not find me. While you are magnificent, by comparison she makes you seem plain and pedestrian. I never thought I would say that about you, but you need to know how I feel.

I know I have hurt you. You deserve someone better than me, and I'm just trying to do the right thing for both of us. It may be difficult, but go into the office tomorrow with your head held high, like nothing's happened. You are forever in my heart, just not in my mouth.

All the best,
John

Tequila Añejo
100% de Agave
11 ELEVEN YEARS RESTED

Los Americanos, New York City

Introduction

> *"Mezcal is one of the world's great spirits: complex, gorgeous and endlessly intriguing, distinguished like great wines by a strong sense of place."*
>
> *Eric Asimov, Food & Wine writer,* New York Times, *2010.*

No, it's really not a goodbye to tequila, just a strong distancing. It is simply hard to get excited about tequila anymore. Once you've been captivated by mezcal's smoky elegance, there is no going back. And for this reason, mezcal is taking the spirits world by storm.

So here we are in 2014. Mezcal can be found—not everywhere—but frequently at places unimaginable five years ago. In New York City, mezcal is at many of the best restaurants in the city: Eleven Madison Park, Daniel, and Gotham Bar and Grill to name a few. It is also featured on the cocktail list at every cocktail bar in the city, and there are a lot of those. Mezcal vending machines are popping up in Grand Central.

This is not a New York phenomenon. Mezcal is happening in every city, big and small, throughout the U.S. You see mezcal-focused restaurants and bars opening around the country. In 2013, we have seen La Urbana in San Francisco and the Pastry War in Houston open as dedicated mezcal bars focused on the spirit and its traditions.

This is happening for many reasons, but at the top of the list, mezcal is authentic. From slow food, to farm-to-table, to the craft brewery explosion, people want something real—not hyped or contrived. Mezcal is real and has nearly 500 years of history. It is hand-crafted and artisanally produced (at least the good ones to which this book is dedicated). It has deep cultural significance in Mexico, from births, to weddings, to funerals, and is deeply woven into the fabric of community life. As people are introduced to the taste of the spirit and begin to understand what mezcal stands for, its popularity will inevitably grow. So why am I writing this book? Several reasons.

1. **I am DEEPLY passionate about mezcal.** My mezcal blog (www.mezcal-phd.com) has been a lot of fun to develop and has become a source (perhaps THE source) of information on the Web for mezcal education. While there are a few books out there on mezcal, there is nothing even close to the type of mezcal book that you or I want to read. I want this book to fill that void.
2. **My wife and my mom.** Are there two better motivators known to man? My wife encouraged me to start the blog and now she, along with my mother, keeps saying, "You should write a book." And I say, "I don't have time to write a book." A weak excuse. Who has time to do anything? So no more excuses.
3. **I have four passions (outside of family):** mezcal, fly fishing, fitness and finance. I can't write books about the other three. I am not a good enough fly fisherman (Mike R. would agree). I definitely am not fit enough (Mike B. would agree). And I underperform the market enough to be disqualified in finance (my broker would agree). Mezcal is all I have left!
4. **The world needs to be exposed to mezcal.** It is little understood. Even the number of bartenders who do not know about mezcal astounds me! Mezcal should be as mainstream as scotch or tequila. That will come in time. This is another step in the journey.

So there you have a handful of the reasons why I am writing this book. If you are a regular reader of my blog you will see a bit of overlap, but I really started this book from scratch and took a fresh approach to what the world needs to know about mezcal—EVERYTHING—as you will see!

I hope you enjoy this journey, and remember to never take mezcal too seriously. **Rule No. 1: Mezcal is fun!**

CHAPTER ONE

What Is Mezcal?

> *"Saying the word 'mezcal' out loud today is like throwing a stone into a pond and watching the ripples spread across the water: It sparks the curiosity of those who hear it, and the interest and passion of those who make it or drink it."*
>
> *Margarita de Orellano*

Mezcal is probably not what you think it is. For most people, if they have any impression of mezcal, it is not a pretty one. It usually involves a worm, a booze-fueled late night and a nasty hangover. In my youth there was a bar in NYC called Lucy's on the Upper West Side of Manhattan. It was packed, raucous and fun. In those days the best tequila you could find was Cuervo Gold. As you know, it is gold in color only, not in quality. You could—and sometimes I would—do shots of Cuervo all night, but that wouldn't earn you a coveted Lucy's T-shirt. If you wanted a Lucy's T-shirt, you had to take it to another level and down a small, two-ounce bottle of potentially terminal liquid that had a suspicious looking parasite in it, and the label said "Mezcal." And this mezcal was DISGUSTING—the retching, burning, gag-inducing ether that you would only imbibe when you were on the outer reaches of rational thought.

If that wasn't enough to keep me away from mezcal, I also thought mezcal was connected to mescaline. Mescaline is a substance obtained from the peyote cactus and it has similar effects to LSD. I now know mezcal is made from the agave plant and has nothing to do with mescaline. Having too much mezcal brings you closer to God, but having too much mescaline makes you think you are a god!

While I still have the Lucy's shirt, my early mezcal impressions began to be reversed in the late '90s and in the last ten years mezcal has earned its

A night I'd like to forget.

way into the respected spirits conversation. Today, if you are looking in the right places, and you should not have to look too hard, you'll see mezcal has rediscovered its historic roots within Mexico and found a willing audience of premium spirits drinkers in the U.S. and abroad.

Mezcal is a beautifully complex and intriguing spirit unlike any other to be found. Of course, I am always asked, "What is mezcal?" Depending on the situation, I may simply say, "It's like a smoky tequila," though I cringe because I am not doing this spirit of the Aztec gods any justice. Stephen Myers from Ilegal Mezcal said it more romantically when he was asked:

> *You know that woman sitting in the corner of the bar? The one with the sultry, smoky eyes. The one that immediately gets your attention and takes your breath away simultaneously? She, who once you are brave enough to introduce yourself to, is smart, clever, funny, intriguing and complex all at the same time. It was just like that with mezcal for me. Mezcal is a complex spirit that the more you partake in the more you learn. There are so many amazing mezcals out there that you are always trying new styles and experiences. I have a strange affinity and love of Mexico and mezcal is such a key part of the fabric of Mexico, its society, history and culture that it truly is a perfect representation of what Mexico really is.*

Yeah. I like that. I might have added, "and it's fucking awesome!"—as long as my ten-year-old isn't around (OK, sometimes when he is, too). You have to experience mezcal. Not everyone takes to it immediately, but like that clever stray dog that keeps following you around, you eventually bring it home and fall in love with it.

Mezcal is a bold spirit. Vodka, the No. 1 spirit in the U.S., tastes like nothing. That's not an insult—it's by design. Tripled distilled, quintuple distilled, google distilled, whatever. All the character of its origination is stripped away.

In fact, the U.S. Bureau of Alcohol, Tobacco, Firearms and Explosives defines vodka as being "without distinctive character, aroma, taste, and color." Mezcal is the opposite. The character of the agave, the fields, the terroir, the wood, the earth, the water, the unique method of production handed down from father to son, from generation to generation, it's all there—in every drop. And it's brilliant.

Now that I've wiped the tears from my eyes, let's look at the elements which factually separate mezcal from other distillates.

TECHNICALLY SPEAKING

Mezcal is any distilled spirit which is made from the agave plant. So tequila is a mezcal. Think of mezcal as the superset which governs all agave distillates, and tequila and other lesser-known agave spirits are the subsets. In Mexico, you hear the term "maguey" (pronounced mah-gay) more than you hear "agave" to describe this plant, but in this book I generally use agave.

We will get into Bacanora, Sotol, Raicilla, Pulque and other agave-based alcohol later in the book, but for now, simply know they are all mezcals.

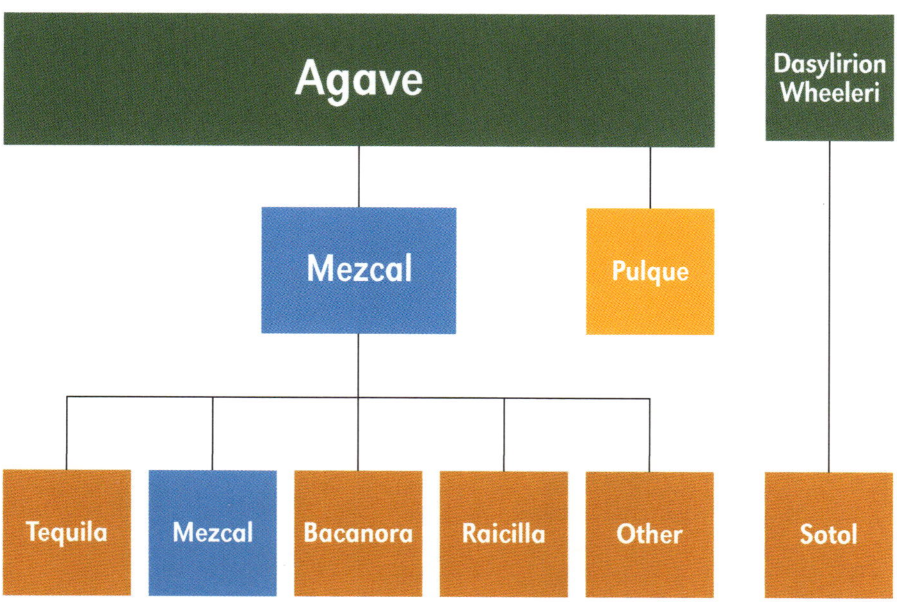

The beginning of the roasting process.

The easiest way to explain mezcal is to contrast it to tequila. There are three key differences between mezcal and tequila which really define mezcal:

1. Mezcal and tequila are made in different areas of Mexico, though there is some overlap. According to their respective internationally recognized Denominations of Origin (DO), mezcal and tequila can only be produced in Mexico. And within Mexico, each DO has specific designated states of production.

   - **Mezcal** can be made in eight specific Mexican states:
     Oaxaca, Durango, Guanajuato, Guerrero, San Luis Potosí, Tamaulipas, Zacatecas and Michoacán

   - **Tequila** can be made in five specific Mexican states:
     Jalisco, Michoacán, Guanajuato, Nayarit and Tamaulipas

   As you can see, Michoacán, Guanajuato and Tamaulipas can produce both mezcal and tequila, as those three states are in both categories. Lots of good things are happening in those states. I should move there.

2. Mezcal can be made from roughly fifty different varieties of agave, while tequila can only be made from the Blue Agave. There is an exciting chapter in your future which goes into all the varieties of agave from which mezcal can be made.

Mezcal Producing States
Durango
Zacatecas
Tamaulipas
San Luis Potosí
Guanajuato
Michoacan
Guerrero
Oaxaca

Tequila Producing States
Tamaulipas
Nayarit
Guanajuato
Jalisco
Michoacan

3. Mezcal and tequila have different production processes which greatly influence the taste of the final product. With tequila, the hearts of the agave plant, known as the piñas, are pressure cooked in large industrial ovens, or autoclaves. For mezcal, those piñas are baked in earthen pits which serve to smoke and caramelize the heart of the agave. The result: Most mezcals have a smoky taste profile, unlike tequila.

Those are the three main differences between mezcal and tequila. Here are a few other important facts about mezcal:

- Mezcal is the oldest distilled spirit in the Americas, dating back some 400 to 500 years.
- Mezcal began to be regulated in Mexico in 1994 under NOM-070-SCFI-1994.
- Mezcal received its international Denomination of Origin (also known as an Appellation of Origin) in 1995, but official regulation and certification of mezcal only began in 2005.
- Mezcal is regulated in Mexico by COMERCAM, an association of producers, brand owners and experts.
- The majority of mezcal is produced in the Mexican state of Oaxaca, utilizing the *Agave espadin*.
- Mezcal exports are approximately .7 percent of tequila exports.
- The agave plant is not a cactus. It is a succulent related to the lily family.
- Mezcal is not an industrial process. It is produced on a palenque, which is a very small distillery (much like a farm minus the chickens, pigs and cows).
- There are estimated to be upwards of 4,000 palenques in the mezcal-making regions of Mexico.

With that, you know more about mezcal than 99 percent of the world. But knowing 99 percent isn't your goal, is it? You want to know it all. That makes us even. The great thing about mezcal is the deeper you go, the more you find you don't know—it cannot be mastered. But it is fun to try. Let's keep trying.

CHAPTER TWO

The History of Mezcal

"You don't find mezcal. Mezcal finds you."

Ron Cooper, Del Maguey Mezcal

Tequila is the spirit most associated with Mexico, but mezcal is the soul of Mexico. It is arguably more culturally significant, though I believe this was lost in much of Mexico's national consciousness during the last 100 years or so. It was only at the turn of this century, during the last decade, that mezcal began to reclaim its rightful place in the cultural hierarchy.

While tequila is more widely known, mezcal came first since tequila is a mezcal. In practice, mezcal was first produced sometime in the mid to late 1500s when distillation was likely introduced to Mexico. Before mezcal, the indigenous people drank *pulque* (pronounced 'pull-cay'), a fermented beverage made from the sap of the agave plant. The drink pulque originates with the myth of Mayahuel.

MAYAHUEL

In Aztec mythology, Mayahuel is the goddess of the agave plant and of fertility (if you are going to be a goddess, those are two great things to have in your realm of influence). As you can see from the photo, she was quite a looker in her day.

As the story goes, Mayahuel got hammered one night and hooked up with Patecatl, who is also an agave god. In the most glorious one-night stand in history, their union produced 400 children! But these were not just any 400 brothers and sisters. They were rabbits. Four hundred rabbit rock stars and fuzzy supermodels promoting madness and mayhem at every turn. My kind of rabbits.

Mayahuel: Apparently she was much better looking in person.

Once born, the little cherubs were fed pulque from Mayahuel's breasts. While unfortunately this image does not seem to depict her 400 breasts, I am sure it made for quite a sight. The pulque made the Centzon Totochtin (400 Rabbits) happy. They were the liveliest, most partying, agave-lovin' drunken rabbits you'll ever know. It is said the Centzon Totochtin are the spirit of the agave and they inhabit you when you get drunk. And, depending on their personality, the type of drunkenness you feel will vary from rabbit to rabbit. Does that mean I have to get drunk 400 times to discover them all? I hope so.

Thus, the tale of 400 rabbits is forever connected to mezcal and tequila, representing all that is good and fun about our favorite spirit. Several bars, which are inviting dens of mezcal and tequila, are in on this myth, including Mayahuel in NYC and 400 Rabbits in Austin.

So that is the story of Mayahuel. It is a good story. *Probably* not true, but good nevertheless. Now let's take a dive into what history tells us.

MAGUEY (A.K.A. AGAVE)

For thousands of years, the indigenous cultures of the Americas have utilized the agave plant as a source of nourishment, clothing, shoes, tools, medicine, construction materials and much more. If you research agave (on a lonely night I presume), you find several references to the Howard Gentry book, *Agaves of Continental North America*, as an excellent source of more information on this topic. If your mission is to learn more about the agaves that are used to make mezcal, you will find it to be a limited resource. Dated and

Rows of agaves can be found all over Mexico.

Latin-geeky, this book was published in 1982. But it is a wealth of information if you simply love agave plants.

Agave is from an ancient Greek word meaning "noble." I cannot think of a more telling linguistic lineage. Just look at it. An agave stands tall and regal, strong and righteous. In the ancient time of the Aztecs it produced pulque, the drink of kings. Agave is part of Mexican heritage and has been a valuable resource throughout the ages.

Agaves are native flora that flourish from the southern part of the U.S., through Mexico and Central America and into South America. They are part of the Agavaceae family, a member of the Liliaceae order, more commonly known as the lily. Agave is not a cactus; it's a succulent. Agave is also found throughout the Caribbean and has been cultivated into Europe, Africa and Asia. More than 200 varieties of agave have been identified, of which somewhere approaching fifty varieties are used to make mezcal.

PULQUE

Outside a pulqueria in Santiago Matatlan

Somewhere along the way during thousands of years of agave use, the indigenous people discovered agave's fermented sap made for a tasty treat. This is pulque. The sap itself, *aguamiel* (honey water), is literally scooped out of the agave plant and then fermented. On a trip to Santiago Matatlan outside of Oaxaca I drank fresh aguamiel from a ripe *Agave pulquero* plant. Indeed, it tasted like lightly sweetened water.

Later, I drank fresh pulque after the aguamiel had been fermented for several days. It was slightly opaque and had a fresh, effervescent citrus-like taste, and was very good. Pulque is alcoholic, ranging from 3 to 8 percent alcohol by volume (ABV), and similar to beer in alcoholic content.

In pre-Spanish Mexico, pulque was consumed by the elite in ritualistic ceremonies. Going to sacrifice a virgin? Give her some pulque to ease the pain—make it a double! Going to marry the daughter of the Aztec king? Make it a triple.

Pulque was incredibly popular for a few hundred years (may we all have a run that good) into the early 1900s. Its popularity declined from there (primarily driven by the growth of the beer industry), though by some accounts pulque still represents about 10 percent of the alcohol consumed in Mexico—doubtful, but stunningly high if true. I have never seen fresh pulque in the U.S. and fresh is the only way to drink it. If you see pulque in the U.S., it likely comes in a can with a disappointing taste. But fresh pulque … amazing.

MEZCAL

Sometime in the 1500s when the Spanish arrived in Mexico, distillation was introduced and the inevitable decline of pulque began. Most historians believe the Spaniards started distilling mezcal in the late 1500s, though they could have started as early as the mid-1500s. The first literary reference to mezcal came in 1621 when Domingo Lazaro Arregui wrote about a beverage being distilled in Nueva Galicia that was clearer than water. Artisanal mezcal has been produced largely in the same manner for more than 400 years and is the oldest distilled spirit in the Americas. Think about that for a second. The mezcal you are drinking today is produced in essentially the same way that has been employed for more than 400 years. If you ever have the chance to visit a truly rustic distillery (and I'm using this word generously) you will confirm this for yourself.

When you see it with your own eyes—the palenque in the middle of nowhere up some random dirt road in the hills of Oaxaca with no electricity or running water and the *mezcalero* (one who makes mezcal) working with clay pots and rudimentary tools—you just *know* he learned his craft from his father and his father's father before him, and you realize they have been distilling this way for hundreds of years. Wow.

Whether it was the Spanish who introduced distillation, or the Filipinos with whom Mexico had lively trading routes at this time, or the indigenous population who actually figured it out for themselves is still a hotly debated topic (yes, some people have a lot of time on their hands). While the academic community continues its attempts to discern the origins of distillation, we celebrate its existence and toast them with a glass of mezcal.

While the precise derivation of the word mezcal is still somewhat unclear, most historians agree that it comes from the indigenous language Nahuatl from the words *metl* and *ixcalli*. "Metl" for maguey or agave and "ixcalli" for cooked. Frequently, you will see the two words combined as "mexcalli." Hence, mezcal is "cooked agave" in ancient Nahuatl.

As mezcal's popularity grew in the 1600s, the wine producers in Spain began to complain about their decline in sales and the Spanish government started to experience an associated decline in tax revenue. In 1595, the King of Spain banned the planting of new vineyards in Mexico, though he said nothing about agave and mezcal. Soon thereafter Don Pedro Sánchez de

Mezcal has been made this way for hundreds of years.

Tagle, a Spanish noble who had immigrated to Mexico, seized the opportunity and established the first agave distillery (rumored to be in the town of Tequila though unconfirmed). He accumulated a great fortune and is known as the "Father of Tequila." But really he is the "Father of Mezcal" because tequila, as a reference to an agave distillate, did not exist until a few hundred years later. That history has mislabeled him is not his fault.

As Pedro and other distillers entered the 1700s, the production of mezcal was actually banned for various periods right up until the end of the century. The cited reasons for this ban had to do with public health concerns. The authorities said mezcal created "moral disorder." God I hope so! Of course, you can't stop progress (or drinking), so while mezcal was banned it still flourished behind the scenes.

As the Spanish were well-steeped in wine production and instrumental in mezcal's development, it was frequently referred to as "Vino de Mezcal" or Mezcal Wine. In 1795, Jose María Guadalupe de Cuervo (yes, that Cuervo) received the first official permit from the King of Spain to commercially produce mezcal under a permit for "Vino Mezcal de Tequila." It was not called tequila then, and not for nearly 100 more years, but since he was located in the town of Tequila the permit was granted as such. So as the 1800s dawned, the ban on mezcal production was lifted and mezcal became more widespread.

For the most part, mezcal production was widespread throughout the 1800s, although a handful of families controlled most of the production. By the mid-1800s, for example, the Cuervo estate reportedly had more than three million agave plants being cultivated. At this point in time, it was all called mezcal. Though much of the production of mezcal was around the town of Tequila, the tequila moniker would not take hold for several more decades.

The name "tequila," representing a regional variety of mezcal, is first found in the tax records in 1873. Also around that time, several of the large producers around the town of Tequila asked the Mexican government if they could officially name their product "tequila" and the government agreed. In the same year the first official shipment of tequila was exported to the U.S., though there is some dispute as to whether Cuervo or Sauza made this move. Though the product was still produced in a traditional mezcal fashion, the tequila handle began to gain traction, and the split between the mezcal and tequila worlds was underway.

The final break between the two worlds came in the late 1800s as the tequila producers in Jalisco stopped using underground ovens and the flavor of tequila was differentiated from mezcal. As tequila production grew, so did the demand for large amounts of wood needed to heat the earthen mezcal pits. Producers realized the substantial deforestation was ultimately unsustainable and introduced large, aboveground industrial ovens as a cooking tool. These ovens needed less wood to cook the agaves, so this path was taken. What this implies about the challenges that mezcal production is facing today is addressed in later chapters.

As the century turned and the 1900s were ushered in, mezcal began to fade and tequila took center stage. I would say that the wrong product won (shocking, I know). But tequila was perceived to be more palatable and less strident in taste. The best product does not always carry the day—the VHS beat Sony Betamax and Windows dominated Apple. And for tequila and mezcal, Cuervo became the gold standard (pun intended).

At this point, I could go on and on about the history of tequila because much has been written. But mezcal? It virtually disappeared from the storyline for the next eighty or ninety years. Mezcal was still being made in the local villages and was regionally significant (primarily in Oaxaca), but tequila and its ability to be produced on a larger scale gained the mind share of both the domestic and international markets. It was not until the 1990s that mezcal began to make a comeback (cue the theme from *Rocky*), as people began to appreciate the unique and historical production process of mezcal.

A young agave field, three to five years from maturity.

CHAPTER THREE

Mezcal Production: Small Nuances Make Big Differences

I asked an old woman what flavors she tasted in mezcal
and she said:
Time.
I asked an old man what is mezcal and he said:
Patience.
I asked a mezcalero what he smelled in mezcal and he said:
History.

It is said that mezcal is the only spirit that is born in a mature state. Unlike grapes, corn, wheat, rye, potatoes and other plants used to make spirits, mezcal is made from ripe agave which can take anywhere from eight years for *Agave espadin* to thirty years for *Agave tepeztate* to mature. Those other crops reproduce at least annually and sometimes more frequently, but agaves only have one shot. At the end of their long lives they are harvested to make mezcal. Think about the life an agave lives before final harvest. You may plant your tepeztate when you are a young mezcalero, but may not harvest it until you are an old mezcalero. Such as it is with mezcal.

The most significant factor influencing the taste of a mezcal is the type of agave from which it is made. There are many other choices a mezcalero makes during the production process to shape his mezcal, but it starts with the agave. The range of flavor profiles is substantial. A mezcal made from espadin is wonderfully approachable with citrus and roasted agave notes, while one made from tepeztate is herbal and musty with notes of wet pavement after a summer rain. The topic of the flavor influences from agave varieties is robust and is covered in the next chapter. Here, we explore the multitude of other influences in the production process which shape a mezcal.

The production process for mezcal is a rich topic, and I won't attack it with glancing commentary—I will go deep. Feel free to breeze through it or move on to the next chapter, but if you really want to "get" mezcal it starts here, for these are the factors that differentiate mezcal from every other spirit on the planet. So immerse yourself and appreciate the seemingly primitive process, because at its core, this is what mezcal is all about.

TERROIR

Loosely translated, terroir means "a sense of place." From Wikipedia: "Terroir is the set of special characteristics that the geography, geology and climate of a certain place, interacting with the plant's genetics, expressed in agricultural products such as wine, coffee, chocolate, tomatoes, heritage wheat, cannabis and tea." The geography of the mezcal-making regions of Mexico is quite diverse, from high desert to semitropical, and ranging from sea level to approximately 9,000 feet in altitude. All of this creates a series of microclimates which change the nature of mezcal from hill to hill and valley to valley. For example, an espadin found in one region compared to another located 200 miles away would result in two different-tasting mezcals even if produced in exactly the same manner. Similarly, two agaves planted on the same day right next to each other may differ in maturity by two to four years. The reason is terroir.

Let's think about wine and the grapes that make it. Wind, rain, slope, sun, soil, hot, cold, humidity, air pressure, elevation and a host of other factors contribute to the grapes' taste for the annual harvest. Now multiply those effects ten to thirty times for the life of the agave. This is all terroir. The mighty majestic arroqueño, mother of *Agave espadin*, can take fifteen or more years to mature. Or the twisting broad-leafed tepeztate which can take thirty years to mature. And it is a path-dependent process: What happens in the first year affects what happens in the second year, and what happens in the second impacts the third, and so on. Stretch that out to ten or twenty years … wow. Each individual agave is different from the one next to it, let alone the whole field, or ridge, or slope across the valley.

Not only do the varieties of agave vary across these areas, but over time, the same agave variety may begin to take on subtle differences in shape, size,

Oaxacan terroir

color and growth cycle, among other things. All of these factors are the terroir at work. The agave plant can take on the flavors around it. Are there pine trees growing nearby? The mezcal may have pine notes. Maybe they are cultivated agaves which are interspersed with other crops such as corn and beans. Over the ten-plus years of the agave growing cycle, these crops will be rotated as well. All of this contributes to and impacts the mezcal.

Other terroir factors are at work as well. Water is used in fermentation and may also be used post-production to lower the ABV of the mezcal. You are unlikely to find the pipes of the Oaxacan Water District anywhere near an artisanally produced mezcal, so the water comes from a well, a river, a stream or perhaps a spring watering hole. Whatever the source may be, it absolutely is part of the terroir and influences the resulting mezcal.

The terroir also impacts the fermentation process. What is the elevation, temperature and humidity of the region? What bacteria are in the air to drive fermentation? Are there fruit trees or other crops near the palenque? As these factors are part of the environment, they too are the terroir.

THE HARVEST

Just like no two agave varieties are alike, no two mezcaleros produce their mezcal in exactly the same way. Small nuances in production methods vary even from father to son, and all choices alter the flavor of a mezcal. But the first step is harvesting the agave.

Left: A quiote growing in the wild.
Opposite, top: Hardworking cortadores harvesting ripe *Agave espadin.*
Opposite, bottom: A freshly cut piña ready for roasting.

When an agave nears maturity, a quiote shoots out from the center of the agave. This flowering stalk can grow up to forty feet tall and signals the end of an agave's life. As the quiote is flowering and drawing valuable starches away from the piña, the stalk is cut to terminate this process and relegate the valuable starches to the heart of the piña. These starches are later converted to sugar during the cooking process and directly impact how much mezcal can be produced from the piña and the robustness of the agave flavor. In the wild, the quiote fully flowers and seeds fall to the ground and take root to produce a new plant. Having produced seeds, the plant will die.

When the *cortador*, one who harvests the agave, is ready to harvest he takes his coa, a long wooden stick with a flat sharp blade attached, and proceeds to chop off the long spiky leaves. He then uproots the piña. Depending on the type of agave, these piñas can weigh as little as ten pounds, such as the wild tobala, to as much as several hundred pounds for *Agave espadin.* Once harvested, the piñas are loaded onto donkeys, wheelbarrows or trucks and taken back to the palenque. The palenque could be nearby or miles away, thus making this whole process back-breaking work. Quality mezcals are not cheap because it is a labor-intensive process.

A typical horno lined with flat volcanic rocks.

The timing of the harvest impacts the mezcal. A hurried mezcalero may harvest his agaves too soon before the quiote develops, likely resulting in a bitter mezcal. Others may believe leaving the quiote stalk intact for an extra week or two before cutting gives their mezcal the right sweetness. Also, once the quiote is cut, the agave may be harvested within weeks or left in the fields for a year or more. The season is a factor as well. Agaves are rarely harvested in the rainy season as the piña swells with water, lowering the yield from each piña. These choices made by the mezcalero are just one more determinant in the development of his mezcal.

EARTHEN PITS

The choice of how to cook agave and extract the sugars is central to the flavor of the mezcal. While not all mezcaleros cook their piñas in an earthen *horno* (translated as "oven"), the majority who produce artisanal mezcals do. This is the way it was done for hundreds of years, as there was no other way. Not until the late 1800s, when technology evolved for the use of industrial-sized aboveground ovens, did the piñas begin to get cooked differently. Tequila

This horno is little more than a hole dug in the ground.

took the quantity approach and left the earthen pits behind. Tequila is the hare. Mezcal is the tortoise. The tortoise always wins—it just takes time. We are 100-plus years behind, but don't give up!

So yes, mezcal producers use hornos to cook their piñas, though not all hornos are identical. How they are used varies from producer to producer. The horno is usually cone-shaped and about ten feet wide at the top, narrowing to a point at the bottom of the pit. As these are simply dug into the ground, the exact size and shape will vary. Size affects the number of piñas which can be cooked at once as well as the time it takes to cook the piñas. This affects the taste. There may be other design features to the horno which influence the mezcal. For example, Eric Hernandez, the producer for Ilegal and a few other brands, has developed a horno with a sub-chamber below the main pit. He built this with an eye toward environmental factors as this structure uses less wood than a traditional roasting pit. But his horno also creates indirect heat which results in piñas that are decidedly less smoky and more evenly cooked.

Some hornos are lined with flat volcanic rocks that serve to retain and intensify the heat. Up in the hills of Sola de Vega—a storied mezcal-making region two hours from Oaxaca City—most of the hornos are not lined with rocks so the piñas abut the earth during the cooking process. Similarly, at the

Wahaka Mezcal palenque in Santiago Matatlan, they told me they do not line their pit with rocks as a terroir choice. They believe there is an eternal connection between the agave and the earth, and the two should not be separated during the baking process. As the earthen-lined hornos generate less heat than a stone-lined pit, the cooking process slows, and this combined with piñas resting against the earthen wall serve to alter a mezcal's flavor. These mezcals have a more gentle and earthy flavor.

The type and amount of wood also influence the flavor. Mesquite, quite common in many mezcal-producing areas, generates more smoke than other types of wood, so these mezcals can be more robust. With growing concern about the dwindling availability of trees, some mezcaleros are now using the fibrous leaves of the harvested agaves to fuel the horno's fire. Some of the more advanced producers are using natural gas to fire their pits.

FIRE VARIATIONS—AND DEEPER WE GO

While the design of the horno clearly affects the outcome, other choices within the pit can substantially change the flavor as well. Once the fire is burning at the bottom of the horno, river rocks are typically piled on top of the fire. After several hours the fire intensifies and the rocks glow red with heat. When the fire is peaking, the piñas are loaded into the horno. Depending on the type of agave used, the size of the piñas varies substantially so sometimes they are placed in the pit whole and other times split or quartered before baking. Tobala piñas, for example, are small and usually placed into the horno intact.

The piñas can be placed directly on the rocks themselves or separated by a layer of moist *bagaso*, the recycled crushed fibers of agave used during fermentation and distillation. (I have also seen this spelled *bagasso*, *bagazo* and *bagasse*.) This layer protects the piñas from the direct heat of the rocks. Some mezcaleros don't use bagaso and place the piñas directly on the wood fire itself, forgoing the use of rocks. Since many piñas are piled into a horno, some get more charred than others that are higher in the pile and have some protection from the direct heat. A mezcal produced with charred piñas will taste different than one where all the piñas are cooked more gently.

At the rustic palenque of Virgillio Garcia Hernandez in Sola de Vega, the piñas are placed directly on top of the wooden fire with no layer of protection.

Top: These tobala piñas were cooked with bagaso protecting the piñas—note the even charring.
Bottom: These piñas were placed directly onto the fire in the horno resulting in a wide range of charring on the piñas.

The roasting piñas are buried under a tarp and earth and left to cook for three to five days typically.

Many of the piñas are completely blackened and charred, but his mezcal is surprisingly balanced and not the smoke bomb one might expect. He knows what he is doing. At other palenques where bagaso is used to protect the piñas from excessive charring, the piñas will come out uniformly cooked across the entire horno. Different styles and different results.

Once all the piñas are loaded into the horno, they are typically covered with more bagaso, burlap or other fibrous material. The mound may reach five to ten feet above the surface before it is covered. After the piñas are covered, a foot or two of soil is added to encase the entire oven. The result is a sealed, earthen oven that will bake the piñas for a few days to a month depending on the season, the piñas and the mezcalero.

In still another variation, some mezcaleros leave a hole in the top of the earthen-covered pit as a design feature. The hole can release heat, and water can be poured down upon the roasting piñas. This configuration moderates the heat and charring of the piñas. The water also creates steam inside the oven, adding a different element of flavor to the cooking process. At the end of the baking process, the starches in the agave have been converted to sugars and the roasted agave is ready for crushing.

Mezcal is smoky, as we all know—sometimes robustly so, sometimes subtly. The common perception is all the smokiness comes from cooking in earthen pits. However, there is another factor which plays into the smokiness of a mezcal. When distillation is taking place at a palenque, smoke is everywhere: smoke from the horno if a fire is in process and smoke from the wood used to heat the still. Even if no distillation or other fire is prevalent, the air is still ripe with smoke and roasted agave. It is in the ground, the air, the wood, the plants, the trees—even the mezcalero! This smoke in the air *infuses* the mezcal with smoke. As the mezcal exits the still with each distillation, it reaches the smoky air and takes on some of this ashen smell and taste. At very small palenques, the horno is usually right next to the still and frequently these mezcals will be even smokier. So yes, the caramelization of the piña in the horno adds to the smokiness of the mezcal, but it is not the only contributing factor.

When the roasting process begins, the air is ripe with smoke.

A mound of well-roasted agaves.

POST COOKING

Once the agaves are cooked, there are a number of subsequent steps which influence the taste of the mezcal. First, the length of time the piñas are left to sit before being mashed is a factor. Are they crushed immediately after they have cooled, or are they left for days or weeks where bacteria may develop as they begin to "rot"? Do you want your mezcal made from a rotting piña? Surprisingly, the answer is maybe! Keep in mind, it is eventually distilled so this production choice is not like leaving a slice of pizza on your countertop and deciding to eat it a week later. Another mezcaleros' choice is whether to peel some of the char off the piñas. By leaving or removing some of the outer char, the mezcalero affects the flavor of his mezcal.

A traditional mill using a horse-drawn tahona to crush the cooked agave.

CRUSHING AND FERMENTATION

Most artisanal mezcals are made by crushing the piñas with a *tahona*, a large stone wheel attached to a central axle which is pulled around a circular stone cylinder by a horse, mule or donkey. Some mezcaleros raise the back-breaking bar further by smashing the piñas by hand with mallets in a wooden "canoe" or similar container. Producers who hand crush are likely doing it for economic not traditional reasons. Horses, grinding mills and tahonas all cost money and many mezcaleros cannot afford it. Regardless of how the agaves are crushed, the resulting mash is called the bagaso and is loaded in the fermentation vats with water. Vats can be made of stone, cement, wood, plastic, or even animal hides if you want to go old school.

Opposite, top: When you cannot afford a horse and a mill, you do it the very old-fashioned way—swinging a mallet. Note the fermentation tank exposed to the elements.
Opposite, bottom: Mezcaleros working the manual process.
Above: The fermentation vats at Real Minero.

I recently acquired a bottle of Vino de Mezcal, a very limited-edition series offered by the Wahaka Mezcal team and sold to fund its agave sustainability project in Oaxaca. This particular bottle is from a very traditional producer in Sonora who is located outside of the mezcal and bacanora DO, so he must use the unappealing label Destilado de Agave, or "Agave Distillate." The fermentation for this Agave lechuguilla-based mezcal takes place in a cowhide stretched over four stakes to create a bowl. The bagaso is placed into the skin where it ferments for about a week. Fermenting in a cowhide does interesting things to the mezcal's flavor, imparting a subtle leathery taste and toning down the mezcal. Not like Grandpa's loafers, but a gentle taste that adds complexity. Also, the type of still utilized in this case is listed as a "modified truck radiator." Only in mezcal....

A fermentation tank beginning to bubble—the yeasts are working.

Another factor, and part of the terroir, is the influence of wild yeasts in the region. Tequila, for example, generally uses cultivated yeasts in a very controlled environment. The fermentation process for mezcal in the open air of the palenque is anything but controlled. What is the elevation? The season? The neighboring crops? What other factors affect the bacteria in the air that aid the fermentation? For example, Cotija, a hard cheese from cow's milk, is made in the Mexican state of Michoacán. Some say that the mezcals made in this region have a dairy-like taste originating from the airborne yeasts produced by the cheese! Personally, I have not been able to identify those flavors, but it makes for a good story (not to mention a good quesadilla).

During fermentation, the water added may be spring water, well water, river water, or whatever water source is nearby. Mezcaleros use the water which is available and this affects the taste of the mezcal. The period of fermentation varies based on season, geography, temperature, humidity and a variety of other factors. Also, if the water is heated before being added, the fermentation process is accelerated. At the end of fermentation the mixture of water and crushed agave is called *tepache*, and is about 8 percent alcohol by volume. Next the tepache is loaded into the still.

DISTILLATION

Once the agave has been harvested, cooked, crushed and fermented, it is on to distillation. Mezcal must be distilled at least twice to be certified for export. I know of a few mezcals which are distilled three times, but most are distilled twice. Increasing the number of distillations may sound appealing, but with further distillations a spirit becomes more and more tasteless. If you compare a mezcal that has been distilled twice to one distilled three times, you find less agave taste in the latter. It may taste smoother because the flavor has been "dampened" by the third distillation. The thrice-distilled mezcal isn't necessarily better than the other, just different.

The type of still used has a significant impact on the taste of any distillate. Tequila is mainly an industrialized process using huge column stills that work continuously, as opposed to one batch at a time. Many tequila aficionados feel these column stills have reduced the veracity of the product over time.

Mezcal, on the other hand, is typically distilled in relatively small copper or clay pot stills which can only produce one batch at a time. The alembic still was invented in AD 800 by a thirsty Egyptian alchemist and brought to Mexico by the Spaniards in the 1500s. Clay pot stills are smaller and found with greater frequency the farther you go from Oaxaca City, as these regions are typically more rural, less populated, and have fewer resources. Clay pot distillation was likely developed after the indigenous population (most likely the Zapotecs) learned distillation techniques from the alembic stills of the Spaniards. Today, many bottles of mezcal specify the type of still used in production. Does clay versus copper matter in terms of taste? Absolutely! Mezcals made in clay pot stills typically have a more earthen quality, while alembic mezcals are crisper and cleaner. Of course, there are so many other factors affecting the taste, these are not universal truths, just experienced observations.

In general, clay pot-distilled mezcals are more expensive because they tend to be very small batch productions and therefore harder to find. Mezcaloteca, a nonprofit mezcal tasting den in Oaxaca, told me they sell clay pot-distilled mezcals as quickly as they come in the door. In the U.S., Real Minero and Siete Misterios are two brands that use clay pot stills and can readily be found online. They are not necessarily better, just different—and pricey. And you can actually taste the earthiness of the clay.

A traditional clay pot still setup.

At the previously mentioned palenque of Virgillio Hernandez, clay pot stills are utilized with an exceptional system to collect the alcohol vapors from the still. In the spirit of resourcefulness, Virgillio uses an inverted metal construction helmet to condense the vapors. The helmet is set upside down on top of the clay pot and it has tubes running cool mountain stream water in and out of the helmet. The vapor condenses on the underside of the helmet and drips through a bamboo rod into a collection vessel. I tasted his mezcal out of an empty Coke bottle and it was transcendent. I asked Virgillio how often he replaces the helmet, and he said every time they pave the road. He lives on a dirt road.

Do not be put off by the sometimes rudimentary process of mezcal production. Certainly it is part of the charm, but it is also regulated and hygienic. The mash is boiled, condenses into vapor, and ultimately the product is lab-tested and certified before bottling. So while mezcal production is decidedly old school, it is perfectly safe.

Virgillio's vapor collection system. The fire is in the brick oven below the pots. The bagaso is loaded into the pot and the inverted helmet is placed on top. Rubber tubes bring cool water in and out of the helmet. As the vapor rises inside the pot, it condenses on the underside of the cool helmet. Then it drips down onto a small bamboo collection plate and streams out of the still. The liquid is mezcal.

When distinguishing mezcal from tequila, some people think mezcal is only distilled once. Perhaps this gives them a romantic and rougher image of the perceived edginess of mezcal, but it is simply not true. Mezcal must be distilled at least twice to be exported, and besides, the 20 to 30 percent ABV of the first distillation is not very tasty. Depending on either the desired taste profile or economic constraints, the mezcal may be diluted with water after the second distillation, resulting in reduced ABV. Some consider the lower ABV mezcal less intense and more palatable. To be certified, a mezcal must be at least 36 percent ABV and as high as 55 percent.

Most mezcals found in the U.S. range from 40 to 50 percent ABV. A high ABV mezcal does not necessarily taste too strong or overpowered by alcohol. Some brands like Del Maguey, El Jolgorio, Pierde Almas and Siete Misterios, to name a few, produce mezcals in the high 40s that are amazingly refined and delicious.

There is an important concept that defines the quality of the spirit known as "the cut." In a distillation process, not all alcohol coming out of the still is

Left: A "modern" artisanal mezcal distillery. **Right:** Rustic, very small batch distillation.

uniform: There is the "head," the "heart" and the "tail." The head is the first alcohol coming out of the still when the vapor starts condensing and contains undesirable flavors, smells and chemicals. The heart is the sweet spot mid-stream where the distillate is most pure and the tail contains a high percentage of fusel oils which impart bitterness to the distillate. Fusel is German for "bad liquor," so yes, we want to keep that out of the mix.

In mezcal, heads and tails translate into the puntas and the colas respectively. So where the mezcalero "cuts" the distillate between the punta, heart and cola defines the quality of the mezcal. Recall that the mezcalero typically has no modern devices to determine where to make his cuts; experience, taste and smell are his tools. Frequently the cut is a demarcation point between a good mezcal and a poor mezcal. For economic reasons a mezcalero may choose to use more of the head or tail in the final product—more head or tail, more booze to sell.

MODERN PALENQUE DISTILLATION

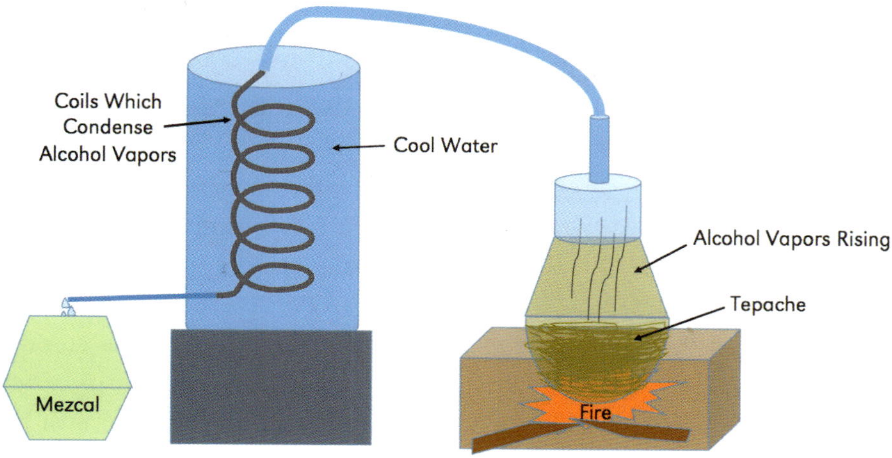

At more modern distilleries, the still is typically copper, or alembic, and has a metal or steel cap which channels the vapors into a cooling tower which condenses them to mezcal. While more efficient, the equipment is expensive.

RUSTIC PALENQUE DISTILLATION

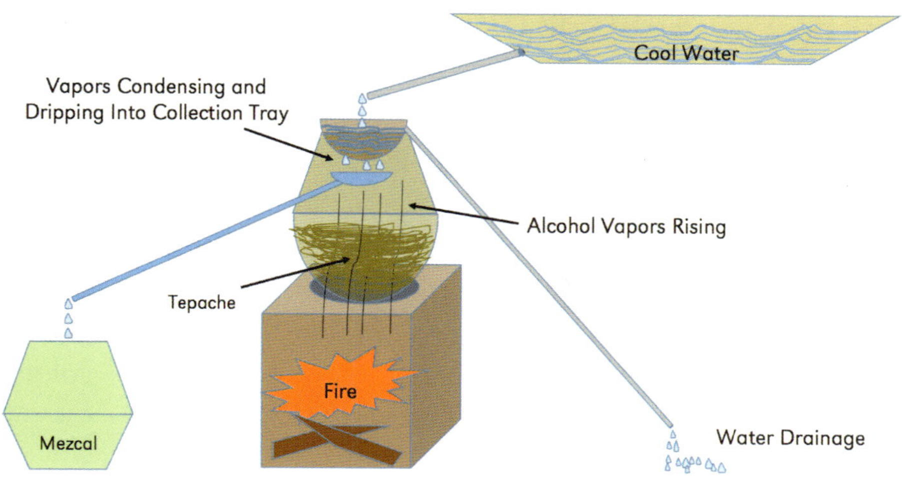

This is essentially the system used by Virgillio. Within the clay pot still, the vapors condense when they reach the cool underside of the water bowl — or a construction helmet in Virgillio's case. The dripping mezcal is collected on a makeshift tray and flows out of the still to a collection pot.

A mezcal tank with the COMERCAM seal on the spout.

Once the distillation is complete, the mezcal is frequently stored in large plastic containers while it awaits COMERCAM certification. The plastic tubs are cured with the tails from the distillation to eliminate any potential plastic smell or taste. COMERCAM places a seal on the spout of the storage container while the product is being analyzed. It must be lab-tested and certified before bottling. Virtually all certified producers have small labs to measure the chemical makeup of the mezcal and to confirm the mezcal is safe for consumption. This process does not fit the romantic image of mezcal, but is part of the certification process to insure a quality and nonlethal product. The sealed container can only be opened with COMERCAM present, after which the mezcal is bottled.

LAS PERLAS

Las perlas (the pearls) are used to judge the alcohol content during and after distillation. They are the bubbles that form when the mezcal is streamed into a container or shaken in the bottle. The size and rate of dissipation of the bubbles tells the mezcalero the ABV. Take a bottle of water and shake it and you'll see a circle of bubbles form a ring against the walls of the bottle. Those bubbles disappear immediately. But with a spirit the bubbles are larger and more enduring depending upon ABV. The optimum range for mezcal perlas is roughly between 45 and 55 percent. I say roughly because the range floats a bit depending on whom you talk to. But generally the bubbles are small and disappear quickly below 45 percent or above 55 percent ABV.

I tried a yet-to-be-diluted 62 percent ABV (holy crap!) mezcal in Santiago Matalan and the mezcalero shook the bottle to show me the virtually nonexistent perlas. Then we went to his final product which was 51 percent ABV—the same mezcal only diluted with water—and gave the bottle a shake. The perlas were big and persistent. An ABV between 45 and 55 percent has perlas that are large and will last ten seconds or so.

A 49 percent ABV mezcal freshly streamed into a small cup—note the size and quantity of the bubbles.

During distillation the mezcalero checks the ABV by sucking mezcal into a bamboo tube and then streaming it back down into a gourd or similar container. He observes the size and dissipation rate of the perlas and correctly assesses the ABV, usually within a 1 percent range. This tells him where he is in the process and whether further distillation is required. If he is satisfied with his mezcal, it is bottled as a joven, or put into barrels for aging.

AGING

Aging is a controversial topic in some mezcal circles, and is discussed more thoroughly in Chapter Thirteen. For now, I will stick to the basics.

Just like tequilas, mezcals can be aged to *reposado* and *anejo* levels, though unlike tequila mezcal does not have an official "extra anejo" category. Reposados are aged a minimum of two months and a maximum of eleven months (though technically eleven months and twenty-nine days seems to qualify). Anejos have to be aged at least a year. As the spirit interacts with the

Barrel aging at the Ilegal palenque.

wooden barrel, chemical changes occur through oxidation and the extraction of elements from the wood. There are many factors affecting the aging process: the amount of charring in the barrel, previous uses of the barrel (perhaps the barrel had been used to age cognac or wine), the temperature and humidity in the aging environment, and the amount of time the mezcal spends in the barrel. The longer the aging process, the more spirit is lost to evaporation. Approximately 10 percent of a spirit will evaporate for every year in the barrel, another reason why aged mezcals are more expensive. This spirit lost to evaporation is called the "angel's share." For deeply aged spirits, the angels have it good.

Of the seventy or so mezcal brands found in the U.S., about a quarter of them offer aged varieties. By comparison, the vast majority of tequila brands offer reposados and anejos. I love many of the aged mezcals on the market. Like any product, some are better than others, but I find many of them to be exceptional and they extend the reach of the mezcal category.

As mezcal is certainly an acquired taste for some, an initial reaction for a new mezcal drinker to a robust joven might not be pleasant. Several years ago as I was getting deeply into mezcal, my wife was no fan. I kept insisting this spirit is amazing while she kept insisting it tasted like a doctor's office on a good day, or dirty socks on a bad day (nice visual, right?). How she knows what either of these tastes like, I don't want to know. But in any case there was no convincing her. Then in late 2009, Ilegal came onto the scene with its reposado and anejo which were the first aged mezcals I had seen in the U.S. My wife, having virtually sworn off mezcal for all eternity, instantly took to the anejo and declared it magnificent! After I picked myself up off the floor, I knew there was another path to developing a mezcal palate. Now, of course, she'll take a daily joven arroqueño IV-drip, but she may have never found mezcal without an anejo introduction.

A fine anejo mezcal may be much gentler on the palate with perhaps hints of vanilla and caramel while still maintaining a subtle smoke and agave presence. Even today, I frequently introduce people to mezcal with an anejo, usually Ilegal or Sacacuento—both are brilliant. So that is what I mean by expanding the mezcal category. A person may initially be turned off by a smoky joven, yet love a reposado or anejo. And then you've brought another convert into the mezcal world!

So yes, I strongly support aged mezcals and I enjoy them on a regular basis. You will too if you don't already.

Viewed from above, an apple-filled clay pot still with a wrapped chicken breast suspended in the well.

The pechuga breast after distillation.

PECHUGA

In Spanish, *pechuga* means breast, and there is a strange but unique distillation process which involves a pechuga. You might think I am teasing you, but no, pechuga mezcals are real and delicious. So what is a pechuga?

After a mezcal has been distilled twice and is finished, it is redistilled a third time by loading wild and seasonal fruits and nuts into the still while suspending a raw, clean, skinned chicken breast (most typically) within the still so the vapors pass over and through it before condensing back to alcohol. The savory breast counteracts the sweetness of the fruit leaving a mezcal unlike any other. Pechugas are polarizing and not for the faint of heart in most cases. They can also be made with turkey breast, rabbit breast, deer meat, or others, and sometimes no protein at all—they are all called pechugas. Also, many Mezcaleros make their pechugas after the first distillation which keeps the agave presence more prominent.

While the precise origin of this distillation technique is unclear, many consider it to be a nod to ancient sacrificial rituals. In traditional ceremonies, if you were a virgin, you were lucky if only a chicken was sacrificed at the altar, as usually that was the minimal offering to the gods. In later years, pulque was frequently colored and flavored with chicken blood. By the time distillation began, it was only natural that a chicken was "sacrificed" in the production of mezcal as pechugas have always been associated with ceremonies and made to celebrate special occasions.

CHAPTER FOUR

Agave Varietals and How They Influence the Taste of a Mezcal

Mezcal is an acquired taste. But a taste worth acquiring.

As grapes are to wine, agaves are to mezcal. Just as a wide variety of grapes produce an expansive range of flavors in wine, so does a broad array of agave species, sub-species, varieties and sub-varieties produce a disparate range of flavors in mezcal. The type of agave used in mezcal production has considerable impact on the taste, and each is unique in its own way. Some are spicy and robust, others earthy and dusty, still others floral and fruity, and some are any combination of these. Mezcal is real and authentic—it comes from the noble agave. It is honest and made by hard-working mezcaleros who have honed their craft over generations. Michael Jackson said it well in the Complete Guide to Single Malt Scotch:

> *The universe of spirits began to change when the word "designer," having become an adjective, attached itself to the word "vodka." Then, some of the most famous names in the world of distillation became better known for their "ready-to-drink" confections, misleadingly known in the United States as "malternatives." Now a new generation of consumer faces a choice between drinks that come from nowhere, taste of nothing much, and have a logo for a name; and drinks that come from somewhere, have complex aromas and flavors, and may have a name that is hard to pronounce.*
>
> *Such drinks reflect their place of origin. They have evolved. They have a story to tell. They are good company, and they require something of the drinker in return; that he or she experiences the pleasure of learning to drink. Real, evolved drinks begin as the gift of God. They are grown,*

Cultivated *Agave espadin.*

whether from grapes, grain, sugarcane, or, for example, the agave plant. They arise from their own terroir: geology, soil, vegetation, topography, weather, water, and air.

Thank you, Michael. Mezcal is exactly as he describes: It has a rich history, admirably reflects its place of origin, and asks the drinker to appreciate its complexity. All of which is driven by the noble agave.

AGAVE

We begin with the type of agave—everything in mezcal begins with the type of agave. There are more than forty varietals from which mezcal can be made, perhaps more than fifty. Some take a relatively short time to mature while others take more than a quarter-century. Some are low, flat and broad in shape, while others are striving skyward with twisting angular leaves clinging to the sides of cliffs. Some, like the tobala, are small and frequently found in the shade of oak trees, making only one liter of mezcal per piña. Others such as espadin can grow very large, eight to ten feet tall, with piñas weighing a hundred or more pounds and producing fifteen liters per piña. In a later chapter, I explore the plethora of varietals in great detail.

Let's think of the different tastes that can be bestowed on mezcal from the unique varieties of agave as a bell curve (finance geeks love bell curves!). A bell curve is helpful because it allows you to visualize the spectrum of mezcal flavors. While this is not exactly a proper use of a bell curve, it is a handy way to visualize the tastes that are comparatively different or elevated. So think of this as a taste curve where the middle represents the most common and palatable expressions of mezcal, and as you move out or away from the center the flavors shift. For example, you will see wild espadin above cultivated espadin as I find wild espadin mezcals to be a bit more interesting and a more intense expression of the espadin norm.

I believe mezcals made with *Agave espadin* represent the standard yardstick of a base level mezcal. That does not mean espadin mezcals are average in taste, but rather mezcals made with espadin are a great benchmarking tool from which to compare the broader mezcal spectrum. Certainly, espadins are the most common, but they are far from uniform. From the skill of the

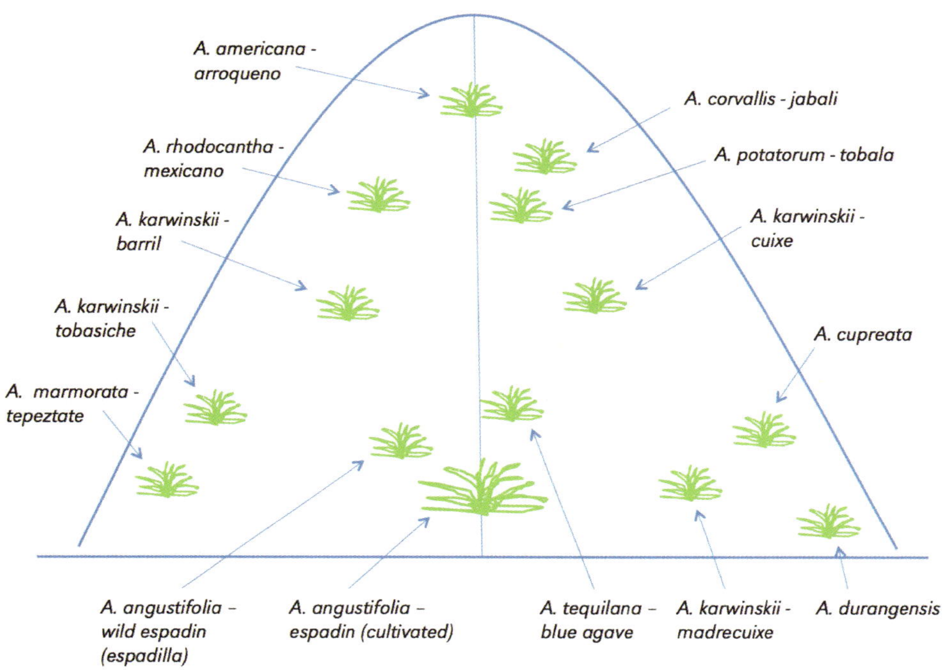

A member of the prolific *A. karwinskii* species—the varietal tobasiche.

mezcalero to the terroir to the fermentation process, many factors affect the resulting mezcal. Some espadins are far better or far worse than others. Still, for flavor comparisons, they are a launching point.

So, you find *A. angustifolia - espadin* sitting on the center line. It is bigger than the others since somewhere around 80 to 90 percent of all mezcals are made from espadin. Above it and just right of the center line of taste is the blue agave, from which all tequilas are made. While mezcals made from the blue agave are uncommon, a number of excellent bottles can be found such as Del Maguey's San Luis del Rio Azul. I hesitate to put it above espadin, but I do find these mezcals a shade more interesting and complex and therefore slightly divergent from the benchmark.

When you try a mezcal for the first time, one of two things is usually present: either a strong, roasted agave taste or a herbaceous, green agave taste. They are separate and distinct, and it is typically one or the other. From there, the flavors that shine through vary widely: ripe banana, citrus, earth, ash, clay, wood, pepper, chili, brown sugar, caramel, mint, pine, anise, floral and mango, to name a few. But again, it starts with the type of agave used. Let's look at some of the other flavors imparted by certain agaves. Back to the bell curve....

Near the tails of the distribution are *tepeztate, tobasiche, durangensis* and *cupreata*, with *madrecuixe* in the neighborhood as well. These mezcals are out there. They are bold and polarizing. Initially, most people love them or have a puzzled look on their face when tasting them. They are just so *different*, and if you are not accustomed to them, you may not know what to make of that first taste.

A. Americana var. oaxacensis, sub-varietal coyote.

Tepeztates are strong on the nose with a pronounced herbal scent—almost marijuana-like in some cases (if you drink enough of it, the effects may be similar). The herbal quality continues on the palate accompanied by rich roasted agave. As your mezcal palate develops, you are likely to find yourself drawn to tepeztates. The *karwinskii* group includes *madrecuixe, barril, cuixe, tobasiche* and *bicuixe* among others, typically delivering an aroma of mustiness. Here, the fruits are more prevalent on the tongue with a long and lovely finish. The overall effect tends to be quite different from espadin but excellent. Even within the karwinskii species the flavors are vastly different. Tobasiche is less elegant and much rougher than a madrecuixe, for example, while barril and cuixe have an elevated simplicity. *A. durangensis* is different from all of the above—mineral flavors with anise and earthiness—and many mezcal lovers (myself included) struggle with it.

As we move back toward the center of the curve, there are *wild espadin, mexicano, tobala* and *coyote*. Wild espadin mezcals are distinctly sharper than those made of cultivated espadin, yet they are still very near the center benchmark. Similarly, a mexicano mezcal is smooth and lovely to drink, but you may notice a bit more complexity entering into the equation. A tobala, frequently referred to as "The King of Mezcals" for its rarity and fullness of flavor, is also near the center line but very elevated in taste. While all mezcals within a specific varietal can vary widely, most tobalas are bright, floral

Top: *A. tobala.*
Above: *A. rhodacantha, varietal mexicano de campo* differentiated by the yellowish leaves.
Opposite: *A. covallis, sub-varietal jabali.*

and full of fruit like mango, plum and bananas, and almost always very easy to drink.

Finally, at the top of the bell curve, near the center line, there are *arroqueño* and *jabali*. I have a strong positive bias toward arroqueños and find them to be amazing. While very complex, they are also incredibly tasaty, which puts them on the center line. They are fantastic, like a turbo-charged espadin: full of roasted agave, bananas and gentle peppery flavors. There are only a few arroqueños on the U.S. market, but a couple I adore are from Siete Misterios and El Jolgorio. They are fairly high in ABV, but still lovely and as approachable as your mother on Thanksgiving.

Jabali is quite similar to the arroqueño with wonderful fruit and citrus tones and nice viscosity. While I have had a few in Mexico, they are currently unavailable in the U.S., but I included it because a mezcal made with jabali is fantastic and I am certain one will be arriving in the U.S. soon.

There are a lot of generalizations here. One of the fabulous things about mezcal is that two different mezcaleros using agaves from the same field may produce completely different mezcals—no two production processes are identical. So not all arroqueños, for example, are sitting near the top of the center line. You may find an arroqueño mezcal which is far afield from a benchmark taste. Revel in these differences and seek them out, as this is just one more reason mezcal is fascinating!

ENSEMBLES

You also frequently find mezcals that are combinations of multiple varieties in the same bottle. These are all "ensembles" and the types of agave used are usually listed on the label. Occasionally the percentage of each agave utilized is specified as well. Many ensembles include cultivated espadin with specific wild agaves. "Espadin is the referee," Paco Garcia from Wahaka Mezcal says. "Mezcaleros commonly use espadin to balance the more pronounced flavor of stronger tasting agaves." And this has been going on for centuries as ensembles have an appreciable place in mezcal's rich history.

Wahaka's Ensamble.

Wahaka makes a beautifully balanced ensemble with espadin, madrecuixe and tobala. Los Danzantes distillery, makers of the brand Mezcalero, releases new blends every six months or so, and they are different every time. There are plenty of other examples. Ensembles can be brilliant and creative bursting with flavor and complexity. Also, as your mezcal palate evolves you will be surprised at your own ability to detect the specific varietals in the blend.

So as you explore mezcal, note the type of agave in every bottle you try. Over time consistent themes will emerge and your palate will sharpen. And if it doesn't, just make it up—your friends will never know.

CHAPTER FIVE

Mezcal Legitimization Begins

Tequila is to wake the living. Mezcal is to wake the dead.

Mezcal disappeared from the national consciousness in Mexico for the better part of a century. Tequila dominated and became the national drink. Internationally, tequila gained its Appellation of Origin (basically a Denomination of Origin, or DO) on April 13, 1978 from the World Intellectual Property Organization. This protected the term "tequila" and specified it could only be made in Mexico. An agave-based spirit could be made in South Africa, for example, but could not be called tequila. Even though various rules and regulations guiding domestic tequila production had applied for thirty to forty years, the DO started tequila down a path toward international acceptability as a quality spirit. But it would take almost twenty years from this point for the perception of tequila to change, which has ultimately been important for the growth of mezcal.

The recognition of the DO for tequila was one key step toward the legitimization of the product. Another important piece of the puzzle was the internal regulation of tequila production within Mexico. On March 31, 1978, the Norma Oficial Mexicana (Official Mexican Standard, or NOM) was put into place to set standards for production, bottling, labeling and quality among other things. While the Norma has been updated and replaced over the years—most recently in 2005—the regulation set the table for sales growth that continues to this day. Regulation creates quality control and gives importers, distributors and ultimately consumers the confidence that they are getting an authentic product. By the way, that doesn't mean it is good (see Gold, Cuervo), just that it was produced to some minimum, nonlethal standard.

With both the DO and the Norma in place by the late '70s, tequila production and sales began to march steadily upward through the '80s. In 1988, Sauza was acquired by Pedro Domecq, precursor of Allied Domecq, the first

Mezcal regions have unique geographical characteristics.

significant tequila brand acquisition by a large international spirits company. In 1989, Patron was founded and became the first aggressively marketed premium tequila. So as the '90s blossomed, tequila's profile elevated with sales rising accordingly.

Down in Oaxaca, a number of savvy mezcal producers were watching the positive economic impact that tequila sales were having on Jalisco and other states. But mezcal was still in the relative dark ages, with no international presence and a reputation as a poor quality spirit even within Mexico. Mezcal was barely treading water because there were no production or other standards applied by the Mexican government and there was no international recognition through a Denomination of Origin. There was a lot of bad mezcal on the market. So these producers began to organize and push for mezcal regulation and an international DO.

They wanted a specific international designation providing the product with a measure of protection and prestige. A designation would certainly help it succeed commercially as it did with tequila, and also bring recognition to mezcal's culture, history and extraordinary uniqueness to the region. These producers also wanted to rid the market of poor quality mezcals that did not meet any standard. So the campaign to legitimize mezcal was launched and it began with the pursuit of a Denomination of Origin.

THE APPELLATION OF ORIGIN/ DENOMINATION OF ORIGIN

An Appellation of Origin is granted by the World Intellectual Property Organization under the Lisbon Agreement, which is an international agreement that protects and designates that certain products can only be made in specific designated areas. The criteria for an appellation of origin are:

- First, the appellation of origin should be the geographical denomination of a country, region or locality. This means that it must consist of a denomination that **identifies a geographical entity in the country of origin**.
- Second, the appellation of origin must serve to designate a product originating in the country, region or locality concerned. So in addition to identifying a place, the geographical denomination must be known as the designation of a product originating in that place—**requirement of reputation**.
- The third requirement concerns **the quality or characteristics of the product** to which the appellation of origin relates. The characteristics must be due exclusively or essentially to the geographical environment of the place where the product originates.

This all makes sense to me and hopefully to you as well. What types of products are granted an appellation of origin? As mentioned, tequila received its appellation of origin in 1978. Other products that have it include champagne, Gruyere cheese, Prosciutto di Parma, many French wines, Cognac, Chianti and many others. Once a product receives an appellation of origin, it can only be made in a specific place. Sparkling wine made in California cannot be called champagne. Mezcal can be made in Arizona, but can't be called mezcal. Got it? So the appellation of origin is *hugely* important in protecting both the cultural aspects of a product and its commercial potential.

The Mexican Institute of Intellectual Property, which is the institution in Mexico authorized to declare protection of an appellation of origin within the country, granted mezcal its appellation of origin on November 28, 1994. Following that, the World Intellectual Property Organization granted mezcal its appellation (appellation of origin No. 731 in the Lisbon database if you are going deep with me) on March 3, 1995. So some say mezcal got its appellation in 1994 while others say 1995. I believe 1995 is the one that counts since it received its international stamp of approval on that date. Finally—and a minor point, perhaps—a Geographical Indication (GI) is a subset of an appellation of origin, and in Mexico a GI is recognized as a Denominacion de Origen, or DO. While some people, including me, refer to mezcal's DO instead of appellation of origin, the two are essentially the same and can be used interchangeably.

Wow. Nerdsville. And finally, the mezcal DO is somewhat controversial in Mexico because it originally included only seven states in Mexico (now eight) that may produce an agave distillate called "mezcal." Although there are at least eighteen other Mexican states that have been making mezcal for hundreds of years, they were excluded from the DO. Why? A bunch of political B.S. as far as I can tell, but that's the way it went down. Now that we are steeped in appellation of origin knowledge, let's continue the story.

THE NORMA (MEZCAL LAW)

Once mezcal received its DO it became subject to a governing law known as the standard Norma Oficial Mexicana NOM-070-SCFI-1994, which includes the DO. This law sets forth a variety of the rules and regulations governing many aspects of the product. While there is a bunch of stuff about packaging and labeling, even I could not get that geeky on you. So let's look at the relevant stuff:

- It lays out the criteria for the three categories of mezcal:

  Mezcal Joven. Unaged and of clear color. Joven means "young" and is akin to a silver, or blanco, in tequila. It is unaged, going more or less from the still to the bottle.

Mezcal Reposado. Reposado means "rested." It is aged two months to less than one year in oak and is light caramel in color.

Mezcal Anejo. Anejo means "aged." It is aged for a minimum of one year in oak in containers limited in capacity to 200 liters and is dark caramel in color.

- In addition, any of the three above categories can be altered to create an *abocado.* The mezcal law allows flavorings, sweeteners, colorings and other additives, like worms, to be added to mezcal, and the resulting product is called an abocado. Strangely or appropriately, if you use Google Translate and type in "abocado" it translates as "doomed." You can't make this stuff up.
- It sets the range of alcohol by volume for mezcal to be 36 to 55 percent.
- While there are three categories (Joven, Repo and Anejo) it also delineates two Types:

  Type I: Distilled from 100 percent agave.

  Type II: Distilled from minimum 80 percent agave and maximum 20 percent of other sugars.
- Interestingly, the Norma does list five types of agaves that can be used for mezcal production. More importantly, it also allows for other types of agave that are not used as the principal ingredient for another DO beverage within the same state. For example, you can use the blue agave to make mezcal as long as you are not making that mezcal in one of the five DO tequila states. This is important as it basically means mezcal can be made from almost any type of agave, which is consistent with what has been going on in local villages and palenques for hundreds of years.
- The regulation and oversight of the Norma is controlled by COMERCAM, and products without its official label cannot be sold.
- There are various chemical requirements that have to be tested in a lab.
- Mezcal must be bottled at the distillery (unlike some tequila which can be shipped in bulk and bottled elsewhere).

As I said, there is more, but these are the most important factors (unless you are a brand, producer, packager or bottler of mezcal).

A nice collection of joven mezcals

COMERCAM

In 1994 when the mezcal Norma came into existence it was not ready to be enforced, therefore at this point in time it was merely a suggestion. But it got everyone moving in the right direction as all producers knew enforcement was coming soon—well, not too soon, as this is Mexico after all. In 1997, an industry regulatory body was established to apply the law. The regulatory body is known as COMERCAM (Consejo Mexicano Regulador de la Calidad del Mezcal A.Ç., or in English, the Mexican Council for Quality Regulation of Mezcal). COMERCAM is an association of mezcal producers, brand owners and experts. In 2003 the Norma became law and COMERCAM began to officially certify producers in 2005. Since 2005, only mezcal bearing the COMERCAM label is officially marketable.

So although mezcal received its DO in 1995, it has only been regulated and certified since 2005! The first official producer of mezcal, Eric Hernandez, who has NOM No. 1, was only certified in 2005, though he is a third-generation mezcal producer.

There is a survey taken in 2005 that illuminates what the certification process can do to legitimize a spirit. In 2005 only 23 percent of Mexicans believed mezcal to be a quality product. By 2008, that number was up to 41 percent! A dramatic improvement in three years and it started with certification.

In the next chapter, I explore many other contributing factors to the relatively recent surge in mezcal's popularity.

CHAPTER SIX

The Rise of Mezcal

If you drink too much mezcal, you don't get drunk.
You get closer to God.

I live in NYC and have been a passionate premium tequila lover for close to twenty years. As the premium tequilas (I am not talking about only-margarita-worthy Patron) really started coming to market in the late 1990s and early 2000s, I went deeper into great tequilas. When my wife dubbed me a "tequila collector" I felt I had license to really go nuts and the bottles began to pile up!

But mezcal in the late '90s and first half of the 2000s? It barely existed, and I didn't own one bottle. I would dabble—and I loved it—when I saw a bottle of Del Maguey, but that was rare. Even by the mid-2000s, mezcal was still undiscovered. So seven or eight years ago mezcal was virtually unheard of and could rarely be found in any bar or liquor store. Thankfully, now you don't have to look that hard as you can find it at most liquor stores, bars and restaurants—at least in New York City.

I don't want to overstate the case because mezcal is still being discovered, but it is everywhere compared to being nowhere only five years ago. So what has happened in these intervening years to take mezcal to near mainstream?

CERTIFICATION LEGITIMIZES MEZCAL

I point to the official regulation of mezcal producers as the primary factor behind the rise of mezcal. However, it is only one of many factors and far from the entire story. I have a theory about how the regulation and certification of mezcal was the catalyst for its rise, but first let's look into certification and its significance.

I have already gone into depth on how and when mezcal reached certification status. Most importantly, mezcal certification only began in 2005. Think about the path tequila traveled. Tequila received its DO on April 13, 1978, and it took at least twenty years for tequila to be perceived as a premium spirit. I say at least twenty years because tequila's reputation is still evolving today, almost forty years since regulation began. All too many consumers still think of it as shots followed by prayers to the porcelain god. So if you wonder why mezcal has become popular only in the past few years, the answer starts here: It barely existed until 2005.

A CONFLUENCE OF EVENTS DRIVES MEZCAL OUT OF THE SHADOWS

Certification and regulation put the framework in place for mezcal's launch. Let's consider what I believe to be a few other contributing factors.

- **Entrepreneurs and Capital.** Being an entrepreneur myself (and therefore confessing a bit of a bias on the importance of this issue), I believe the most important outcome of certification was the emergence of a fertile environment for entrepreneurs, which includes enterprising producers. Certifying the product is expensive and many mezcal brands and producers simply cannot afford it. Even after certification, capital is required to create a brand, produce it, bottle it, label it, export it, develop importer and distribution agreements, and market it in the destination markets. Passionate mezcal entrepreneurs have stepped into this arena because they have capital (well, barely), vision (occasionally), energy and enthusiasm (always), and abilities (sometimes) to create a business with the producers. While I do not know the origins of all the brands that are commercially available, I know many of them have been brought to market by entrepreneurs who partnered with quality producers.

  Some people might not appreciate this, disparaging the commercialization of mezcal and the pursuit of profits by entrepreneurs. But many of these entrepreneurs are producers themselves, have created jobs in Mexico and the U.S., and have brought recognition and awareness to our favorite spirit. They have also stayed true to mezcal's hand-crafted production. The other important element the entrepreneurs bring is evangelical passion. They love mezcal deeply, so it is not just a commercial enterprise for them. Thus the entrepreneurs, in my view, gave mezcal the initial boost post certification.

- **Mixology.** To me, the mixologists followed entrepreneurs into the fray. A better characterization is that entrepreneurs *dragged* mixologists into the arena. But man, once the mixologists got there, they lit it up! I am not sure mixologists would have ever discovered mezcal were it not for the entrepreneurs and their legions who were out pounding bars and restaurants on a nightly basis to encourage the recognition of this beautiful elixir.

  Of course, mezcal arrived on the scene in the late 2000s as the cocktail craze was in full swing so this helped. As the mixologists discovered its smoky elegance, they embraced its inclusion in cocktails. In NYC circa 2009, you rarely saw mezcal on a cocktail menu. By 2011, you could barely find a cocktail menu without a sexy mezcal concoction. The entrepreneurs started it and the mixologists gave mezcal accelerated visibility. But still there were other factors.

- **Cultural Rediscovery.** With certification, a cultural renaissance of mezcal began in Mexico. The survey I cited earlier regarding mezcal's perception within Mexico drives home this point. Certification provided legitimacy and prestige, and Mexicans began to rediscover their cultural roots as they relate to mezcal. Mezcal is part of their national heritage. It was the first distilled spirit in the Americas and has been a part of the Mexican culture for almost 500 years. It is used in celebrations for births, weddings, funerals, baptisms, birthdays and virtually every other important milestone that you can think of. This went on for hundreds of years, but somewhere in the 1900s this crept into the background. Maybe it was the worm, maybe it was the times. But somewhere in there, mezcal developed a less-than-stellar reputation and the pride for this artisanal, beautiful and historic spirit dissipated. So again, it seems that certification unearthed a few historical and cultural roots. Today, mezcal is all the rage in Mexico. In Mexico City, high-end mezcal bars are everywhere and even the finest restaurants now have deep mezcal selections. People are proud that this fantastic spirit is part of their heritage.

- **Generational Shift**. This theme lives comfortably with Cultural Rediscovery and is an idea put forth by Steve Myers from Ilegal. As premium tequilas grew popular, tequila itself enjoyed a bit of cultural rediscovery. During this period in the mid to late '90s and carrying into the 2000s, tequila became the drink of the establishment in Mexico. Simply stated, it was what your father drank. When mezcal hit the scene in the mid-2000s, the young saw it as a way to embrace their heritage but not follow their parents' path. So young crowds discovered mezcal and helped drive it to new heights—nowhere more so than Mexico City.
- **Artisanal Demand and Premium Products.** In the past ten years or so, "artisanal" and "artisan" became new marketing buzzwords—some authentic, some questionable (see Domino's "Artisan" Pie or Tostitos Artisanal Chipotle Chips). But thankfully, many people cannot be fooled and they look for truly artisanal products. That mezcals are not mass produced like many tequilas began to filter into the mezcal story. While mezcal has relatively high price points to evidence that fact, it also has the quality people expect from artisanal products. Mezcal is authentic and fits well into rising demand for small batch, organic, farm-to-table, hand-crafted, boutique and less industrialized food and drinks. Think about the craft beer movement and the rediscovery of American Rye and small batch whiskeys, like Hudson Whiskey. The sales of these products have exploded in the past decade. This current has also contributed to the growing popularity of mezcal. Mezcal is made on farms, not factories.

These are some of the factors that I believe have been integral to the rise of mezcal. Here is a summary: **Check out my groovy graphic.**

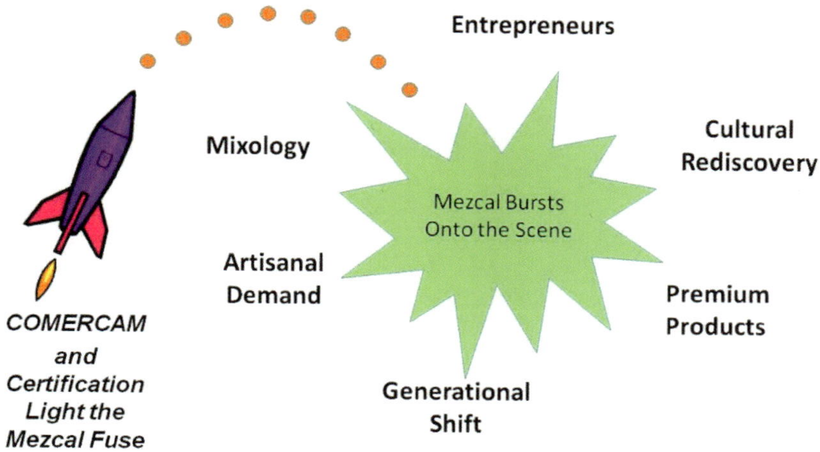

While mezcal is taking off (like a rocket, get it?), let's not get ahead of ourselves. Mezcal is still *tiny* compared to tequila. For every bottle of mezcal sold in the U.S., about 150 bottles of tequila are consumed. Mezcal is still shockingly small. For now....

SnANDRÉS
MEZCAL
48.1% ALC. VOL.
MEZCAL
Alipús
MEZCAL
JOVEN 100% AGAVE
PRODUCT OF MEXICO
MEZCALES DE LEYENDA
GUERRERO
USDA
ORGANIC
mezcalero
Net. Cont. 750 ml
2013
001- ARQ
264/ 300
MEZCAL JOVEN
PEDRO VASQUEZ O.

CHAPTER SEVEN

Of Mezcal, Tequila, Sotol, Raicilla, Bacanora, Pulque and More

"Everybody's got to believe in something.
I believe I'll have another drink."

W.C. Fields

As you certainly know by now, any *distilled* agave-based spirit is a mezcal. So under the broad category of mezcal are a variety of spirits that are unique in their own right. Also in the general family of agave-based alcohol there is pulque, which is derived from the agave but is *not distilled*. Beyond tequila and mezcal, these spirits are not widely known. Though as the growth of tequila and mezcal continue, the other agave spirits may slowly seep into the consciousness of agave connoisseurs.

Before we get into some detail, here is the basic schematic from Chapter One of what this world looks like.

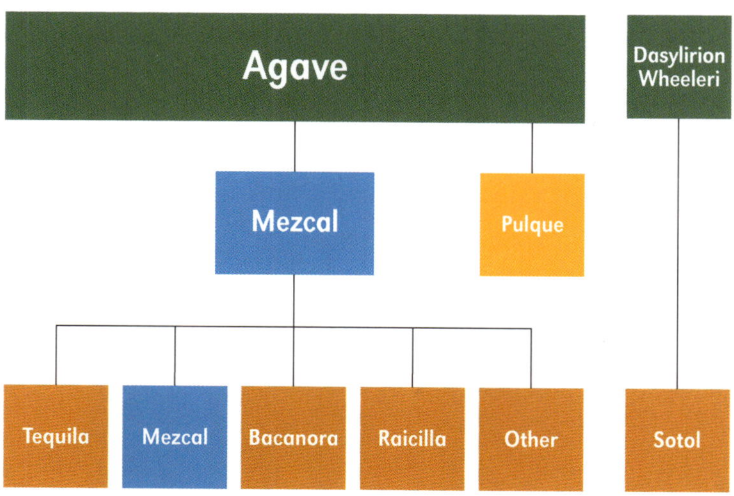

At the top, there is Agave (which we know comes from the Latin word meaning "noble," so it belongs at the top). Directly below Agave is Mezcal, the category that envelops all spirits that are distilled from the agave plant. Then mezcal has sub-categories below it. I also put mezcal as a sub-category of itself, because the bottom row is really how people think about the world of agave distillates.

At the top and to the right is Pulque. Pulque is also derived from the agave, but it is not a distilled beverage. And to the far right there is *Dasylirion wheeleri* from which sotol is distilled. Why is it here if it is not an agave distillate? Because most people think it is an agave distillate since *Dasylirion wheeleri,* known as the Desert Spoon or Sotol plant, used to be in the *Agavaceae* family (the botanical agave family). Taxonomy, the branch of science concerning the classification of organisms, is far from locked down and organisms frequently get reclassified. So, as it is very closely associated with tequila and mezcal, its inclusion in this discussion is important.

Let's take a look at all the categories with a handful of the distinguishing characteristics of each:

MEZCAL

- Mezcal is any distilled spirit made from the agave plant.
- So technically tequila, bacanora and raicilla are all mezcals.
- Mezcal has an internationally recognized Denomination of Origin (granted in 1995), which means that mezcal can only be made in eight designated regions of Mexico.
- Mezcal has been regulated within Mexico since 1994 and is overseen by COMERCAM, but only since 2005 has mezcal been officially certified.
- Mezcal can be made from any type of agave with enough sugars to produce alcohol.
- There are roughly fifty different varieties of agave that can be used to make mezcal.
- Mezcal is typically produced by baking the hearts of the agave, or piñas, in earthen pits, which imparts a smoky flavor to the mezcal.
- There are approximately seventy mezcal brands currently being imported into the U.S.

TEQUILA

- Tequila can only be made from the Blue Agave (*A. tequilana*).
- Tequila has an internationally recognized Denomination of Origin (granted in 1978), and can only be made in five designated regions of Mexico.
- The regulation process for tequila began in the 1940s within Mexico, but the NOM was first passed in 1978 and has been periodically updated over the years.
- Tequila is regulated within Mexico by the CRT.
- Tequila can be as little as 51 percent agave with up to 49 percent corn, sugarcane or other alcohol, but all the good ones are 100 percent agave.
- With tequila, the hearts of the agave are typically pressure cooked in large industrial ovens, known as autoclaves, which do not impart any special flavor characteristic to the resulting tequila.
- There are about 1,000 tequilas imported into the U.S.

SOTOL

- Sotol is made from the *Dasylirion wheeleri*, or Desert Spoon, also known as the sotol plant. *Dasylirion wheeleri* is a stem succulent related to yucca and agave. It was formerly in the agave family but now is classified as a member of the *Nolinaceae* family according to The Succulent Plant Page (and many others), and thus sotol is not a mezcal. I suspect people in Mexico really could not give a crap about this technicality ("Hey Juan, can you believe this shit? They changed the freaking taxonomy!!??"), so I include it here as it is closely associated with mezcal.
- Sotol has a Mexican DO, granted in 2004, not an international DO.
- The sotol NOM, regulating production, etc., was passed on April 15, 2004.
- Sotol is regulated within Mexico by the Consejo Mexicano de Sotol (formed in 2004), and can only be produced in the Northern Mexican States of Chihuahua, Coahuila and Durango.
- The few commercial sotol producers only use wild sotol plants, which take fifteen years to mature.

Ocho Cientos Sotol — new to the U.S. in 2014.

- It generally takes one plant to produce one bottle of sotol (compared to tequila or mezcal where one plant can produce five to ten bottles, though there are exceptions).
- The piñas can be cooked in aboveground ovens and distilled in column stills, like the Hacienda de Chihuahua brand, or produced more like a Oaxacan mezcal with earthen pits and copper stills, like new arrival Ocho Cientos.
- There are only a handful of sotol brands imported into the U.S. with Hacienda de Chihuahua, Don Cuco, and Ocho Cientos being the most notable.

BACANORA

- Bacanora is produced from the wild *Agave pacifica*, also called *Agave yaquiana* (*A. angustifolia*), or simply bacanora, a plant that grows in the mountain range of the State of Sonora, which is the only region where bacanora can be produced.
- While the DO specifies *A. angustifolia*, in practice *A. vivipara* is used as well as are other closely related agave varietals. It seems some producers consider the DO to be more of a guideline in this regard.
- Bacanora is a mezcal. It has a terroir largely to its own in the mezcal world due to Sonora's arid climate and relative elevation.
- Bacanora is named after the town Bacanora, which is in Sonora.
- It was illegal to produce bacanora from 1915 to 1992 due to some messy issues that sprang from the Mexican Revolution in the early 1900s.

Naturally, much production continued though it went underground.

- Since November 6, 2000, bacanora has had a Mexican DO, but not an international one.
- The bacanora NOM, regulating production, etc., was passed on October 28, 2005.
- Bacanora is regulated by the Consejo Sonorense Promotor de la Regulacion del Bacanora, formed in 2006.
- There are regions in Sonora that are not in the bacanora DO, so they cannot label their distillates bacanora in those regions.
- Like mezcal, the hearts of the piña are roasted in earthen pits imparting a smoky flavor to the final product. Sonoran piñas are much smaller due to the lack of rainfall in this arid climate.
- I only know of one bacanora brand that can be found in the U.S.: Cielo Rojo Bacanora.

RAICILLA (PRONOUNCED 'RYE-SEE-AH')

- Raicilla is produced in seven municipalities of Jalisco and is frequently associated with the Puerto Vallarta area.
- Raicilla is primarily made from the *Agave lechuguilla* (*Agave inaequidens*) and *Agave pata de mula* (*A. maximiliana*), and it also goes by its regionally common name, *Agave raicilla*.
- Raicilla is a mezcal, though it cannot be labeled as such since it is not produced in a mezcal DO state.
- Raicilla does not have a DO or a NOM, however since 1997 there has been a collective mark, "Raicilla Jalisco," to protect production.

The hollowed-out center of an *Agave pulquero*. The aguamiel collects in the center and can be scooped out twice a day.

- All raicilla producers must now be members of the Mexican Council of Raicilla Promoters and there are currently around seventy members.
- With raicilla, the hearts of the agave are usually cooked in aboveground ovens so it is not smoky like mezcal (some raicilla producers use earthen pits as in mezcal).
- Perhaps the best known (and I use this generously) raicilla distiller is Destilador del Real, though it cannot be found in the U.S.

PULQUE

- Pulque is not a distilled agave product, but rather a fermented alcohol product made from the sap of the agave. The sap is called aguamiel, translated as "honey water."
- One plant can produce 500 to 1,000 liters (130 to 260 U.S. gallons) of aguamiel over two to six months.
- It is 3 to 8 percent ABV, so similar to beer in alcoholic content.

- Pulque is made from more than ten agave varieties including the appropriately named *Agave pulquero*.
- Pulque has no NOM or DO or anything else.
- The heart of pulque production is just north of Mexico City where the states of Hidalgo, Tlaxcala, and Estado meet, though pulque is made throughout Mexico.
- You can find canned pulque in the U.S., though all reports suggest it pretty much sucks.
- You can get fresh pulque in Oaxaca, but you have to know where to look. It tastes like honey and citrus with a crisp and effervescent finish. It's delicious!

OTHERS

- **Sikua.** Produced in Michoacán, sikua was/is mezcal made in this state before Michoacán was included in the mezcal DO. The sikua nomenclature is seemingly being left behind now since Michoacán can now officially make mezcal–Michoacán was added to the Mezcal DO in 2013.
- **"Destilado de Agave".** In 2006, an "agave distillate" NOM was passed to govern all mezcal-making regions not recognized under a DO. So these regions can make a mezcal, but not call it one. And they are left with the unappealing choice of calling it an agave distillate. Unjust, it seems.
- **Comiteca.** An example of a Destilado de Agave, comiteca is a well-known regional mezcal made in the town of Comitan in the state of Chiapas.
- Some other obscurities can be found here and there, but they are quite far afield.

That is the rundown. Other than potentially raicilla, I do not see any new grants of Denomination of Origin status on the horizon.

We tend to think that agaves only thrive in arid environments.
Here is a wild tepeztate in an evergreen forest at almost 9,000 feet.

CHAPTER EIGHT

The Types of Agave from Which Mezcal Can Be Made

"I drink to make other people more interesting."

Ernest Hemingway

I want to know how many unique varieties of agave are used to make mezcal. This topic is my Achilles' heel. It is my weakness because I cannot fully conquer it, yet I cannot let go of it either. It baffles and confounds the common man and the academic alike (OK, it probably confounds the common man a bit more). The reasons for this are many, but here are a few. First, names for the same type of agave may vary from village to village and region to region. Second, there are naming issues due to the various local languages of Spanish, Zapoteco, Mixteca, and Nahuatl (and a few others) that are spoken throughout the mezcal making regions by the indigenous people. Third, there is a concept in biology known as geomorphism, which basically means that the same plant may take on different characteristics in different areas due to environmental factors or cultivation. They may start out the same, but over time they change and adapt and essentially become a different varietal. Fourth, there are mezcaleros using agaves that are yet to be classified or simply have a colloquial name. Finally, there are botanical names and there are nicknames. The nicknames are used most commonly, and they too vary from region to region—the same nickname frequently represents two completely different agaves. These facts, combined with my inherent lack of botanical expertise, make this a challenging topic. But that has not stopped my pursuit. I have researched exhaustively, contacted well-known academics in the field, and annoyed the hell out of everyone who may be able to provide some agave tidbit.

Why is this important? The single most important factor in the taste of a mezcal is the type of agave from which it is made. One of the most delightful

Wild *Agave tobala* is frequently seen growing out of rocky outcroppings.

mezcal experiences is tasting several different varietals and enjoying the significant variations. In fact, according to my friend Steve Olson (an accomplished spirits industry expert), the best way to taste mezcal is to explore the differences from one expression to the next.

For years, the only varietal regularly seen beyond *Agave espadin* was the Del Maguey Tobala. But in the last few years as mezcal has gained popularity, there has been an explosion of varietals that have come to market. I am not always convinced the introduction of many varietals is positive for the mezcal category, as it may confuse the average consumer (no offense if you are the average consumer—be glad you are not an agave nerd!). Yet for the mezcal enthusiast or budding enthusiast, the varietals are fascinating to explore. As you have seen in prior chapters, there are a lot of varietals out there including tobala, madrecuixe, tepeztate, arroqueño, barril, tobasiche, mexicano, sierra negra, coyote, tripon and cupreata, to name a handful. And the list is much longer as you will see.

Determining the number of agave varietals from which mezcal can be made seems like an easy task. I mean, we are not trying to solve the mystery of Stonehenge. No, I just want to find an answer to a *seemingly* simple question. But if you do a Google search on "Varieties of agave that make mezcal," you will quickly find there is no good information.

Maybe COMERCAM can help? So you look at the mezcal Norma, but find that the Norma only lists five types of agave to make mezcal. However, the Norma allows for other species of agave to be used to make mezcal. This explains why the exact number of agave varieties that can be used to make

Wild *Agave cupreata*, also known as papalome or papolometl.

mezcal is a moving target. I have seen sixteen, twenty-three, twenty-eight and thirty types of agaves from various sources. Also, given that there are estimated to be thousands of mezcal producers in eight regulated states with more than 200 known varieties of agave (though not all 200 have the sugar content to make mezcal), I would bet that mezcal is made with a good portion of these. The vast majority of these producers are small palenques that use the agave found close by. This is just one more thing to love about mezcal—all the answers are not necessarily there. You can't master it.

That said, I feel better knowing that the list continues to evolve, and it is not a fixed number. So I keep digging. But it is a surprisingly complex and confusing topic. I am researching and Googling and my head is swimming with botanistic (is this a word? botanical? botaninistical?) terms such as variety, kingdom, family, genus, species, order and division. My finance degree is rendered worthless in this pursuit. Should I have paid more attention in 10th grade biology?

I needed some academic assistance so I contacted Wendy Hodgson, Research Botanist and Curator of the Herbarium in Phoenix. She provided these clues. The hierarchical taxonomy starts with the *Agavecaea* family, which is the botanical agave family. Below that, there is genus, species, variety, sub-variety and sub-species. For example, if you are looking at *Agave americana L. var. oaxacensis,* she explained *Agave* is the genus and *americana* is what is called the specific epithet, and combined *Agave americana L.* is the species. Sub-varietals may exist beneath the varietal *oaxacensis*. The "*L.*" is a nod to the author of the species name, Carl Linnaeus (who, by the way,

The mighty arroqueño, known as the "King of the Agaves" for its large size.

published his book categorizing many plants in 1753), but the "*L.*" is optional in this case. Also, *Agave* is typically abbreviated "*A.*" and is italicized as I have used throughout this book.

By way of a brand example from El Jolgorio Mezcal, let's look at *A. americana var. oaxacensis*, within which lies the sub-varietal arroqueño. Here: *Agave* is the genus, *A. americana* is the species, *A. americana var. oaxacensis* is the variety, and arroqueño is one of several sub-varieties.

It is becoming more common for mezcal producers to go to great lengths to communicate the contents of their bottle. Most artisanal producers now put the variety on the label. El Jolgorio is one producer that has both the species and the variety on the label. Here is the label:

A. Americana var. oaxacensis is the species and arroqueño is the sub-varietal. My research tells me *A. Americana var. oaxacensis* has other sub-varietals such as sierra negra and coyote, so there are at least three sub-varietals from this specific species of agave. I am looking for the varietal, sub-varietal or sub-species in most cases. Any unique agave and/or varietal from which a mezcal can be made—that is the goal.

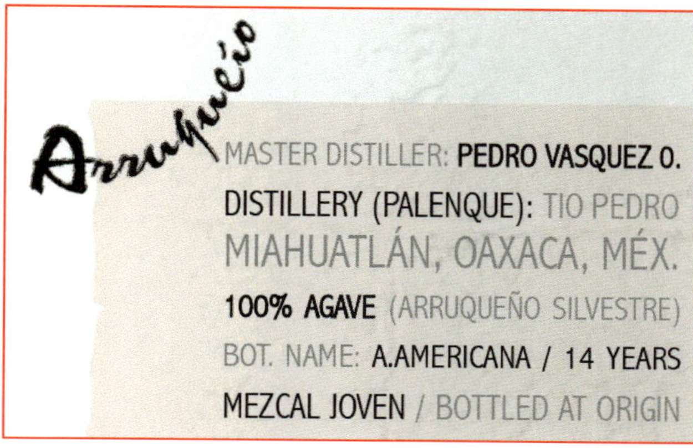

The Master Distiller and where it is produced

100% Agave, and the varietal is wild arroqueño (silvestre)

The botanical name of the agave is A. Americana harvested at 14 years

I also contacted Jorge Larson of CONABIO, a Mexican government agency which among other things has done research on the types of agaves used to make mezcal. He is part of the team that developed Mezcales y Diversidad, which is a beautiful glossy fold out map showing agaves and a variety of granular information on each. Specifically, I asked him his thoughts on the *Agave karwinskii*, as I have twelve karwinskii varietals on my list (meaning I believe there are twelve unique sub-varieties of the karwinskii species from which mezcal is made). I wanted to confirm the twelve sub-varieties as separate and distinct. While he provided excellent information, the core of his response was: "Are they different species, different sub-species, varieties or cultural ecotypes? Who is to know?" And he is an expert! What are the rest of us supposed to do if this is where the experts come out?

Jorge further explained *A. karwinskii* comes in many shapes and sizes with subtle differences between madrecuixe, cuixe, barril and cirial, for example. While some of these may be common and interchangeable names, others may exhibit substantive differences between varietals.

Over the years, as wild agaves are cultivated (i.e. planted and farmed), they begin to exhibit subtle differences from their wild brethren and in some cases morph into a species or sub-varieties unto themselves. In the book *Tequila!* by noted agave scientists Ana Valenzuela-Zapata and Gary Nabhan, they write:

> *In his 1982 masterwork, Gentry recognized that this single, wide-ranging species, which he called Agave angustifolia Haw., was comprised of both wild agave and cultivated varieties. It is one of the few species that*

A. karwinskii, sub-varietal barril.

ranges from the Atlantic coast of Tamaulipas all the way to the Pacific coast of Sonora, and from the northernmost to the southernmost states in the Republic of Mexico.

Got that? Here is the translation. *Agave angustifolia* is *Agave espadin*, from which about 80 percent of all mezcal is made. But it has been cultivated for centuries and over time has taken on an identity of its own while its wild cousins have taken on their own identities, or regional versions of itself. The most significant example of this is *Agave tequilana*, the Blue Weber, used to make tequila of course. Gentry essentially identified this as *Agave espadin*, but recognized that through years of cultivation, it had taken on unique characteristics, and therefore he concluded: "Since these differences are of a degree rather than a distinct contrast, **their separation as a species is nominal, but appears tenable where species are so hard to define."**

So Gentry, the grandfather of modern agave taxonomy, thinks these species are hard to define! What of the poor blogger-turned-author? I have no chance. But I do not accept that—I marshal on, and work on my mezcal-driven agave research with the same passion as Gentry himself!

That all said, I hope you appreciate the scope of the issue as to why the precise number of species, varieties, sub-varieties and sub-species is a moving target. Between regional terminology, botanical morphing, cultivated varieties of wild species and academic inconclusiveness, reaching definitive conclusions is clearly difficult.

A FOOL'S ERRAND

The more time you spend in Oaxaca, the more you realize mastering agave taxonomy is an impossible task. So I think I have a handle on the agaves, the names, the varietals and sub-varietals only to make another stop into In Situ or Mezcaloteca to find more varietals that I have never heard of! It is nuts.

A word about In Situ and Mezcaloteca, both Oaxacan mezcal dens. In Situ is a small bar owned by Ulises Torrentera and his partner Sandra. Ulises and Sandra are giants in the mezcal world for their humility and depth of knowledge on all things mezcal, from the history to distillation to types of agave. Small producers come to them with hope that In Situ will carry their mezcal. Only the finest mezcals are selected, and Ulises puts an In Situ label on the bottle with deep information on the producer, agave,

The bar at In Situ. "Ninety-nine bottles of mezcal on the wall. Ninety-nine bottles of mezcal ..."

The aftermath of another fine tasting at Mezcaloteca.

fermentation, type of still, etc. For these mezcaleros, it is the highest honor for Ulises to pick their mezcal. In Situ has somewhere around 150 unique bottles of mezcal from about a hundred different producers. I ask him how many unique agave varieties are used to make mezcal, and he shrugs. He hasn't really counted and I can see he doesn't really care. He is not brushing me off, the number is simply irrelevant to him. I am so American—I need quantification!

Mezcaloteca takes a different tact. It is an appointment-only, nonprofit cathedral to mezcal combining the words mezcal and *biblioteca* (meaning "library") to create a mezcal library: Mezcaloteca. Beautifully appointed with antiques and green lamps on the bar, it is like walking into a church (bless me Father for I am about to sin). They are a bit dogmatic with a mission to preserve the making of "Traditional" mezcals, which I feel is an unnecessary distinction (more on this in Chapter Twelve), but they are doing God's work by promoting quality mezcals. It is unclear how many bottles they have, but I would guess seventy-five to a hundred unique ones. With deep knowledge, they have walked me through fabulous tastings, and again, introduced me to varietals I have never heard of.

In Situ and Mezcaloteca, combined with the taxonomy challenges and far-flung palenques, make me realize "agave quantification" is a fool's errand. I guess I know what that makes me. The varieties, the subtleties within species, the extensive lack of classification of wild agaves existing in remote hills and valleys, plus cultivated, semi-cultivated and wild versions of the same species all combine to insure a lack of precision in my pursuit. And you know what? I love it. At first it drove me crazy, but now I bow down to Mayahuel and actually appreciate this additional factor in my love for mezcal. If all the agave varieties were known, the thrill of the discovery process would be diminished. The excitement of tasting a mezcal at a palenque in the Oaxacan hills, finding it to be amazing, and having the mezcalero tell me it is from yet another varietal I haven't heard of—for me, that can't be beat.

So I am stating upfront this is not THE list, because there isn't one and probably never will be a complete and fully accurate one. This list is my compilation after much inquiry, research, poking around, a tidbit here and a tidbit there. You get the idea. But I do know that I have not found a more complete list—not even close. Not to say that one does not exist, I just haven't seen it.

As you will see in the table, most varieties, sub-varieties or sub-species are associated with specific brands. However, in some cases when I could not find a specific brand, I did find multiple references to the fact that mezcal is made with this type of agave. I also considered cultivated varieties to be distinct from the same wild species where there appears to be evidence of clear differences between the agaves. So, in my list, it counts as a type of agave from which mezcal is made if I can find a brand or credible reference that says mezcal is made from the species, variety, sub-variety or sub-species. For example, with the species *Agave americana var. oaxacensis*, I find four sub-varieties from which mezcal is made: coyote, arroqueño, blanco and sierra negra.

So here is my official, yet very unofficial list.

#	Agave Species	Sub-Species or Sub-Variety (and Synonyms)
1	Agave americana var. oaxacensis	coyote, chato
2	Agave americana var. oaxacensis	arroqueño
3	Agave americana var. oaxacensis	sierra negra
4	Agave americana var. oaxacensis	blanco
5	Agave americana	americano, mezcal, serrano
6	Agave potatorum	tobala
7	Agave karwinskii	madrecuixe
8	Agave karwinskii	bicuixe
9	Agave karwinskii	tobasiche
10	Agave karwinskii	barril
11	Agave karwinskii	cuixe (Cuishe)
12	Agave karwinskii	tripon
13	Agave karwinskii	largo
14	Agave karwinskii	cirial
15	Agave karwinskii	verde
16	Agave karwinskii	penca verde
17	Agave karwinskii	mexicano o san martin
18	Agave karwinskii	amarillo
19	Agave rhodacantha	mexicana amarillo, amarillo grande, penudo
20	Agave rhodacantha	mexicanito de campo, mexicano de campo
21	Agave rhodacantha	mexicano
22	Agave cupreata papalome, papalote (ref Saldana)	cupreata, ancho, maguey de mezcal, bravo,
23	Agave cupreata	chino
24	Agave angustifolia	espadin
25	Agave angustifolia	pacifica (wild espadin) or rubescens
26	Agave salmiana sub-species crassispina	salmiana, verde, manso, cimarron (ref Saldana)
27	Agave salmiana sub-species crassispina	horse, caballo

Sample Brand	Reference / Comments
Siete Misterios, Vago	
El Jolgorio, Siete Misterios, Del Maguey	
Mezcalero Release #4	
None known	Scorpion website, Sol de Vega
None known	Mezcales de Artes
Del Maguey, Vago	
Yuu Baal, Wahaka	
Mezcalero Release #6, Mezcaloteca	
El Silencio, Pierde Almas	
El Jolgorio, Scorpion, Banhez	
El Jolgorio	
Mezcal Real Minero	
Mezcal Real Minero	
Mezcal Union	
Espiritu Lauro	
In Situ	
Espiritu Lauro	
Mezcaloteca	Yellowish leaves
Siete Misterios	Also used for raicilla
	Sola de Vega palenque
El Jolgorio	Pierde Almas calls this dobadaan
Mezcales de Leyenda	
Mezcaloteca	
Many	In raicilla production also called chico aguiar, pata de mula, lineno
	In the bacanora DO
El Tinieblo	
El Koch	

#	Agave Species	Sub-Species or Sub-Variety (and Synonyms)
28	Agave maximiliana	lechuguilla, manso, tecolote, pata de mula
29	Agave inaequidens	lechuguilla, bruto
30	Agave univittata	estoquillo, mezortillo
31	Agave durangensis	durangensis
32	Agave durangensis	cenizo
33	Agave tequilana	blue agave
34	Agave marmorata	tepeztate
35	Agave de lumbre	de lumbre
36	Agave pasmo	
37	Agave cierago	
38	Agave pasmo y cuelo	
39	Agave esperrima Jacobi	maguey de cerro
40	Agave esperrima Jacobi	bruto o ceniza
41	Agave weberi cela	maguey de mezcal
42	Agave iophanta	estoquillo, mezortillo
43	Agave funkiana	henequen, ixtle de jaumave
44	Agave hookeri	ixquitecatl, mezcal bravo
45	Agave kerchovei	pasmo, jabali, acallo, escobeta
46	Agave palmeri	mano largo, chino bermejo, lechuguilla
47	Agave scabra	bruto, de carro, serrano
48	Agave seemanniana	maguey chato
49	Agave shrevie	mahi totosa, bacanora, ceniza
50	Agave pelona	verde pelona
51	Agave covallis	jabali
52	Agave sierrudito (local name)	
53	Agave liso (or de pita)	
54	Agave pulquero	

Sample Brand	Reference / Comments
None known	Mezcales de Arte, also raicilla is made from this agave
Raicilla El Real	Used for raicilla
None known	Mezcales de Arte
Mezcales de Leyenda	
Mezcal EL Mas Pais	
All tequilas plus some mezcals	
El Jolgorio, Del Maguey	
El Koch	El Koch says species is unclear
None known	Scorpion website
None known	Scorpion website
None known	Benesin website
None known	NOM 70 plus Espiritu Lauro website
None known	NOM 70 plus Espiritu Lauro website
None known	NOM 70 plus Espiritu Lauro website
None known	Academic paper
None known	Academic paper
None known	Academic paper
None known	Academic paper
None known	Zapata. Used in Sonora
None known	Academic paper
El Koch	
None known	Zapata. Used in Sonora
El Koch	
Acquired in Sola de Vega, no brand	Sola de Vega
In Situ	Small with jagged leaves. Not classified.
	Sola de Vega
	Tasted in Matatlan. Used to make pulque.

Wild madrecuixe being harvested by the side of a road.

As discussed in the introduction, there is likely overlap and oversight. Most likely, overlap is the biggest issue. For example, there are a number of agave species where I cannot find a brand using that species or varietal, but I have seen them myself at unbranded palenques or found academic evidence to support inclusion on this list.

Another source utilized is *Mezcal de Artes*. This was a magazine-like article published a few years ago that included the CONABIO map. For several of their species, associated sub-species and varietals, I cannot find any mezcal brands. But the information comes from CONABIO, so the source is good.

For example, I have twelve *A. karwinskii* varietals. Are there really that many or are they simply the same plant given different names in different villages? My research suggests they are different but I still have doubts.

The log-like piña of the madrecuixe after harvest.

At any rate this may not be the complete answer, but should be an excellent guide. As you travel the mezcal world, check the bottle to see what type of agave is used to produce the spirit you are drinking. Be a bit suspicious if you see suspect packaging and no agave varietal listed. I mention packaging because there are a number of excellent mezcals on the market where the packaging is gorgeous, and the mezcal is great, but they do not list the varietal. In most cases, it is because the brand created their label before it became popular to list the varietal.

Finally, I cannot leave this topic without mentioning the *Agave pescador*, or the "fish agave." As I was traveling deep in the hills of Oaxaca, an old mezcalero told me of the intriguing *Agave pescador.* Just before an agave reaches the end of its life, the quiote shoots up from the heart of the agave. The quiote is cut off and the agave is harvested. The mezcalero told me that in addition to making a great mezcal, *A. pescador* has a quiote with a special quality: When tossed into a river, the flowers have a poisonous venom that kills nearby fish, allowing for their easy harvest for a pescador feast. While it made for a great story, I had my doubts.

But after doing further research on the possibilities of this, I discovered an interesting fact. A wide range of special chemical compounds can be found in

The quiote of the mysterious *A. pescador* perhaps?

the leaves of agaves, including saponin. Saponin is a form of steroid that foams when shaken and is generally poisonous to certain lower level animals including fish! Naturally, I was as stunned as the fish by this revelation. These saponins are found in a variety of agaves including *Agave lechuguilla,* which is found throughout Mexico and commonly used in Sonora to make bacanora. While I found no specific reference to *A. pescador* as a varietal of *A. lechuguilla*, it is no leap to imagine the colloquial name given was pescador. And it became known that when *A. pescador* matured, a mezcal-fueled fish fry was about to throw down.

CHAPTER NINE

The Worm and How It Set Mezcal Back Fifty Years

"I always take mezcal at night as a preventive of toothache.
I have never had the toothache; and what is more, I never intend to have it."

Mark Twain (paraphrased)

I curse the worm! Well, OK, that may be a bit dramatic, but I am definitely not a fan of the worm. On second thought, I really do curse it. The only good place for a worm is in the mouth of a fish.

The worm we are talking about is more correctly referred to as a larvae (*gusano* in Spanish), and can be frequently found in a bottle of mostly **BAD** mezcal. There are two types of maguey worms that infest (that's right, *infest*) agave plants: white maguey worms and red maguey worms. Both worms are technically larvae.

The white maguey worms, known as *meocuiles,* are caterpillars of a butterfly. The butterflies deposit their eggs on the leaves of the agave. The larvae then eat the flesh of the agave stems and roots, sometimes boring it out completely.

The red maguey worms are known as chilocuiles, chinicuiles or tecoles, and are the larvae of a moth. These infest the core and roots of the maguey plant, often in a glutinous mass. Who wouldn't want to eat

Red maguey worms at a local market.

a glutinous mass? Let's celebrate these majestic creatures by putting them in the fine spirit known as mezcal.

Yep. So that's what they are. That's what some mezcal producers, but not most premium mezcal producers, put into their bottles. But why? Adherence to an ancient Aztec tradition? Did Mayahuel feed her 400 drunken rabbits a glutinous mass of red agave worms? Nope, nothing like that. You may also hear it is a technique master mezcaleros employ to make sure the alcohol content is just right (if the worm is alive and squiggling, not potent enough; if it is decaying, too strong). Not true either. And then some also say they put the worm in mezcal because the worm, if eaten, has a drug-like or hallucinogenic effect. This too is B.S. There are several legitimate theories about how the worm ever made its way into a bottle of mezcal.

THEORY ONE

Over its hundreds of years of existence, mezcal has been infused with everything from fruit to bark to vegetables to poultry breasts. Even today, while not mainstream, it is not uncommon. At the Wahaka Mezcal palenque, I tried a mezcal infused with apples and another that was gin-like and infused with herbs. Mezcaleros continue to experiment and the results can be fascinating—maybe not always good, but fascinating nevertheless!

Given this backdrop and the Oaxacan fascination with eating crickets, grasshoppers, ants and worms, mezcal historians (yes, they exist) believe mezcals *con gusano* are perfectly consistent with Oaxacan culture. While there is little in historical literature to support the widespread use of worms, it seems logical that mezcaleros might drop a maguey worm into a bottle.

THEORY TWO

The modern history of the worm in a mezcal bottle may have more to do with American than Oaxacan culture. While there is debate as to precisely when and who started this, many people attribute the worm apocalypse to a Mexico City entrepreneur, and now brand owner of Gusano Rojo mezcal, who hit upon the idea as a marketing gimmick to attract more attention to his mezcal (where were the *Mad Men* when we needed them?). Apparently it worked with the American tourists and many other mezcal producers followed suit. In fact, it worked too well, as this habit was adopted by subpar mezcal brands and mezcal became known as a bad spirit with a worm in it. The early mezcals that reached the U.S. all had worms and U.S. tourists also returned from their vacations believing that mezcal, 1) tasted like crap, and 2) had a worm in it. Mezcal has been living down this reputation for fifty years.

THEORY THREE

During World War II, tequila enjoyed a huge surge in demand in the U.S. due to the lack of whiskey coming in from Europe. The Jalisco tequila producers could not handle the demand so they looked to their counterparts throughout Mexico for additional production. Most of these producers had neither brands nor labels so their products were non-descript. U.S. importers began to complain as they wanted to know if the spirit had come from Jalisco or elsewhere. The Oaxacan producers started putting a worm in their bottles so the importers would know it came from Oaxaca. This theory is plausible because the timing coincides with the establishment of several large mezcal brands including Monte Alban and the previously mentioned Gusano Rojo.

Top: Sal de Gusano with orange slices.
Above: Fried grasshoppers are in abundance at the Oaxacan market.

TODAY

Thankfully, mezcal's reputation has changed and now the worm is rare in quality mezcals. The few quality brands which have a gusano version believe in the cultural significance of the worm, and do not do it for marketing purposes. I wish even the quality brands would not do it. There may be a cultural reason to do it, but I feel it reinforces the negative mezcal stereotype that most everybody else is trying to live down. I understand why Toby Keith at Wild Shot puts a worm in his (something to do with the fact that he knows little about even his own mezcal), but the premium brands? I wish they wouldn't.

SAL DE GUSANO

There is one good thing, however, that the worm is used for: *sal de gusano*, or "worm salt." Initially you may be repulsed by worm-laced salt, but once you try it you may be surprised.

In Oaxaca, a traditional way to sip mezcal is with an accompaniment of orange slices and sal de gusano. The salt is made by combining crushed red worms, chili powder and salt. It tastes like spicy salt and pairs beautifully with orange slices to cleanse your palate between sips of mezcal. You can try this yourself at many fine Mexican restaurants that feature mezcal, as they serve mezcal with a side of oranges and worm salt. You can also buy it online at The Meadow (www.atthemeadow.com) among other places. Although buying sal de gusano outside of Mexico is very expensive, it is almost free on the streets of Oaxaca.

If you are a bit nuts and happen to be looking for other insect varietals to try with mezcal, buy sal de chapulin ("grasshopper salt") in Oaxaca. It pretty much tastes the same, and you can tell people how open-minded you are.

CHAPTER TEN

The Future of Mezcal

"If I had to live my life over, I'd live over a saloon."

W.C. Fields

SUSTAINABILITY

The future of mezcal is bright in so many ways. But the sudden and rapid growth of mezcal creates specific challenges. Agave is not grapes or wheat or rye or corn or Jägermeister or anything else grown in a short period of time (I am not sure how fast Jägermeister is grown, but I am thinking minutes). Spirits made of these agricultural products can meet demand through rapid expansion and turnover of crops. Agave is more challenging.

A row of *Agave angustifolia*, variety espadin in Oaxaca.

Espadin, the most common type of agave used to make mezcal, takes a minimum of eight years to mature and frequently exceeds ten years depending on all the environmental factors that affect the growth cycle. While the long gestation period for agave contributes beautifully to the complexity of the ultimate mezcal, it also means ripe agave cannot be created on the fly. Mezcal is said to be made with four ingredients: agave, sun, water and time. And agave needs a lot of time to grow.

Unlike tequila, mezcal has not reached the stage where millions and millions of acres are dedicated to agave crops. To date, the demand has not been there. With demand rapidly accelerating there is a risk that it may outrun supply and negatively impact mezcal production before sustainable and sophisticated agave crop management finds its way into the mezcal world.

TEQUILA AND MONOCULTURE

For tequila, all blue agave is cultivated. Even that has presented enormous challenges as the reproductive process for blue agave has tended toward what is referred to in botany as "monoculture." As a blue agave reaches the age of three or four years, "pups" start sprouting at the base of the piña. These pups are just baby agaves being seeded by the mother plant, and they are referred to as clones. The farmers tending the fields will uproot these clones and use them to plant the next generation of fields. As this process continues over time, entire fields of agave become genetically identical. While other species of agave produce pups as well, the monoculture issue is most prevalent with blue agave due to the much larger production volume of tequila as compared to other agave distillates.

Consequently, when monoculture crops face adversity from fungus, bacteria, infestation, drought or whatever, all the plants tend to be affected in the same manner. They all catch a cold at once and they may all die at once. A similar field of agaves with a wide-ranging diversity of mother plants would not suffer the same fate.

In the last thirty years or so leading agave botanists have begun to understand this problem and are now creating ways to manage it. In a recent *Bloomberg Business Week* article written by Ted Genoways, he examines the way leading tequila firms are now managing their crops:

> *At the nursery and research laboratory for Beam's Casa Sauza, just outside the village of Tequila, José Ignacio del Real Laborde, the company's technical director, ducks under the wall of a black mesh canopy that spreads for forty acres, shading the 50,000 agave pups growing underneath. "They all look very similar," says del Real, "but there are 400 different mother plants." Del Real is well aware of the concerns botanists, ecologists, and tequila connoisseurs have about his crop.*
>
> *He bends down to a row of agaves, each individually potted, and scoops one up for closer inspection. "What is a plant?" he muses. It's like a remarkable machine, he says, converting the sun's energy and the earth's nutrients into carbohydrates. When both are abundant, the agave will use those carbohydrates for new growth, but during times of scarcity, the plant turns conservative. "So we restrict about 20 percent of the*

light," del Real says, "and the plant knows not to grow large leaves, but instead to store its sugars in the stem."

This small, counterintuitive trick is one of numerous innovations instituted by del Real, who holds a Ph.D. in plant science from Utah State University, since he was hired by Sauza Tequila in 1999. Barrel-chested with thick, expressive eyebrows and a quick wit that bounds between data and philosophy, he has turned the art of agave production into a methodical agriscience, advancing well beyond conventional spray-and-irrigate efforts. Today, all of Sauza Tequila's agaves—some 15 million plants—begin with two to three years in del Real's greenhouse. They're moved to open fields according to a schedule, determined by past productivity of that particular region and company projections of sales over a 10-year period. When the right time is selected, each pup will be planted according to a global positioning system-created map and linked to a log of monthly field surveys. The health assessment of each field then determines a disease-, weed-, and pest-management plan.

Del Real wrote the book, literally, on modern agave crop management, and he has developed field guides for Sauza Tequila's workers: to identify plants they can harvest and eat and to spot and collect flowering plants they can transplant to their gardens. He has spent more than a decade developing pesticide-free management techniques, such as pheromone-baited traps for the agave weevil and the promotion of beneficial insects to reduce fungal infections. Most important, he has established a science-based culture of cooperation, where researchers from major tequila producers—Cuervo, Herradura, Orendain—share knowledge and learn from academic researchers through conferences and jointly published handbooks available to everyone. In a densely packed growing zone, where competitors' crops often share a fence with each other, it doesn't make sense to keep an effective method secret from your neighbor. "If everybody doesn't do it," del Real says, "then we're all going to have trouble."

The high-tech methods used by big producers extend well beyond the fields. Inside Casa Sauza's tequila factory in the heart of town, every industrialized method has been embraced—and it shows in the gleaming stainless steel equipment and nonskid floors painted with caution markers for danger zones. Here agave piñas are pulped in a shredder,

Mezcal remains a hand-crafted process.

carried by conveyers to a "gentle extraction" diffuser (which del Real likens to a coffee brewer), and then steamed in high-pressure autoclaves. The juice, or aguamiel, is then pumped into gargantuan carbon dioxide-controlled vats for fermentation and distilled in 4,000-liter (1,000-gallon) column stills. Sauza Tequila makes no effort to disguise its industrialized product, even prominently marking large holding tanks "corn syrup" in the part of the factory where low-purity mixtos are produced. Indeed, the most disconcerting part of Sauza Tequila's facility is the mechanical roar and general absence of human workers. But to del Real, this is evidence, as he told Wine Inquirer magazine, that their processes "are on the cutting edge of industrial sugar extraction technology."

This is insightful on so many levels. First, it speaks to what a huge business tequila has become. Not that we are surprised, but still this really drives it home. Second, it dispels any romantic notion one may be harboring about the way large brands produce their tequilas. This is big business. Mezcal is nothing like this and let's hope it never gets there.

Not that we need more evidence, but here is a recent Facebook post from a noted mezcal and tequila enthusiast (name withheld):

> *We sat in a room in Philadelphia a few years ago with a powerful executive from a large multi-national corporation who a couple of years before had overseen the acquisition of one of the largest tequila brands in Mexico. We all expressed our concerns about the quality of the product, having noticed significant declines over the past decade. After a back and forth conversation about the legitimacy of these concerns, we did a blind tasting of older and newer products. The results spoke for themselves. The real conversation finally started at that point. I was shocked when this individual, probably the most powerful man I've ever spoken to in the spirits business, told me he had never considered the difference between how tequila and whiskey are made. He was simply applying the same marketing practices his company used for whiskey. He had no knowledge of concerns about sustainability, no knowledge of agricultural cycles, no knowledge of genetic diversity, and claimed to rarely drink tequila. This was the man who made this decision.*

This is tequila today. That said, there are some brands such as Fortaleza, Siete Leguas, Ocho, Tapatio and Excelia that are producing their tequilas in a traditional, non-industrialized way, and they remain excellent. While mezcal is a few decades behind tequila, everything happens more quickly today. Mezcal is currently less than 1 percent of the tequila market, but it is gaining quickly and discussions like this freak me out about the future of mezcal.

Mezcal stakeholders can learn from what has transpired in the tequila industry. Will they? There are two very big issues here, which are clearly linked. First, the agricultural process around how agave crops are grown and managed. And second, what will happen to mezcal when the large spirit companies decide to get involved?

AGAVE CROPS AND SUSTAINABILITY

As discussed, the tequila companies are attempting to manage their crops in a sustainable way. But it is debatable the extent to which they are succeeding in the world of tequila. There has again been an agave shortage in the past two years and many reports of tequila companies "raiding" Oaxaca for large truckloads of espadin. While the tequila companies deny it, many suspect they are using the espadin (someone throw the flag!) to produce tequila as they are short of blue agave in Jalisco. In response to the previously mentioned *Bloomberg Business Week* article, a tequila producer, Marco Tulio Roman of Tequila 3R, wrote:

> *Dear Mr. Genoways,*
>
> *I'm afraid that your report is inaccurate, "Today the tequila industry says it has overcome its boom-and-bust cycle through industrial agriculture and what Eduardo Orendain, president of the National Chamber for the Tequila Industry, calls 'careful planning.' Officials at the chamber point to the current oversupply of agave...???"*
>
> *The Tequila industry is going through another agave crisis during the past two years, currently agave prices have skyrocketed to 500% and this crisis will deepen even more next year. Insiders point that this new crisis will last for another 5 years, until new crops are matured.*
>
> *I'm a Tequilero and I've seen my production prices increased at least 50% in the last year. Unfortunately the industry hasn't overcome "its boom-and-bust cycle" no real "careful planning" has been established. The curse still lingers.*

Thank you Marco for that perspective. But what does it mean for mezcal?

First there is the immediate problem of the agave raids into the official mezcal making regions. But longer term, all parties with a vested interest in mezcal should be thinking about these issues, formulating plans of action and executing steps toward sustainability. The resource issues are not solely agave. Other strained resources include water and wood, which are potential problems as well.

CULTIVATED, SEMI-CULTIVATED AND WILD

Because mezcal can be made from so many varieties of agave, sustainability has many layers. About 80 percent of mezcal is estimated to be from cultivated *Agave espadin*. So the issue here is largely similar to that of the blue agave and tequila. The maturity curve is longer but similar, from eight to twelve years, so crops must be managed to avoid the boom and bust cycles. The reproduction process must also be considered: Are monoculture crops being created or does the crop exhibit biodiversity? To date, monoculture has not been a big issue because the demand for cultivated espadin is not as great as that for blue agave—again, mezcal being less than 1 percent of tequila production.

But clearly it is important for mezcal producers and growers to pay attention and learn from what has happened with cultivated blue agave crop-management techniques—both their successes and blunders.

Another important discussion is taking place around the silvestres, or wild agaves. This is exactly what it sounds like: These agaves grow in the wild. So if nothing is done to improve management of these wild resources, wild agaves will become increasingly rare. Yes, it sounds either blasphemous or incongruous to talk about managing something that is "wild." Clearly it has never worked with Madonna, so why should it work here?

These wild agaves have existed for thousands of years, and they have been able to reproduce and sustain in the wild. But the problem now is the surging demand for these varietals has created a more rapid utilization than these plants have ever seen. Here are a few examples of fantastic mezcals that are produced with wild agaves (and yes, all of these are sold in the U.S):

- Siete Misterios, *Agave arroqueño*
- Del Maguey, *Agave tobala*
- El Jolgorio, *Agave tepeztate*
- Pierde Almas, *Agave dobadaan*

And that is just the tip of the veritable silvestre iceberg. Many brands have a tobala variety, for example, and brands like Del Maguey and El Jolgorio produce silvestres from five to ten other types of agave. Like most silvestres,

A purple-hued semi-cultivated tobala.

these are very limited production runs due to limited supply of wild agaves. I wonder if we will be able to enjoy these and other fine varietals into the future.

Which brings us to semi-cultivated. I would guess without some form of semi-cultivation, many of these wild agaves would disappear or come close to it. I am not a botanist, but semi-cultivation seems like a good plan. Semi-cultivation is when baby plants are raised in a nursery or other structured environment and then replanted in the wild. A good example of this occurred in the summer of 2013 when Pierde Almas sponsored a reforestation of 1,000 baby tobalas. A group of volunteers ventured out into the hills of Oaxaca and planted the little guys in a classic semi-cultivation effort. It was the fourth year in a row that Pierde Almas has run such a reforestation program.

In another semi-cultivation effort, Fundacion Agaves Silvestres (www.agavessilvestres.org), a project sponsored by Wahaka Mezcal, purchased land in Oaxaca and planted fields of tobala and madrecuixe. In a few years each plant will be adopted by a local school child and replanted in the wild. At maturity, Wahaka will buy them at market prices to help fund the schools. Nice.

It is presumed that many of these wild varietals can be cultivated, but in many cases this has not been tested. But, Mezcal Vago has a cultivated tobala

The nursery at Agave Silvestres.

varietal. How does the cultivated tobala taste compared to wild tobala mezcal? Well, Vago is the only cultivated tobala I am aware of, and it tastes completely different from every other tobala I have tried. But, from the maker, there are other factors at work:

> *So that particular tobala isn't wild, it was planted in 1996, making it 17 years mature. It's what we call a bien picado, meaning it has flowered but not yet died, and is more or less overripe. This and Tio Rey's touch (the mezcalero), plus his spring water and 90-year-old fermentation vat, gives this mezcal a flavor unlike any other Mezcal. There are 200 bottles a year available and only for another couple of years.*

How cool is that? This is the beauty and essence of mezcal. The mezcalero overripens his agave. Why? Because he can. Then his unique spring water used in the fermentation process, combined with an antique fermentation vat, produce a mezcal like no other. Most mezcal tobalas are refined, floral, smooth and bursting with fruit flavors. This tobala is rough and earthy, yet wonderfully complex and delicious. It is truly unlike any mezcal I have had. Is it the cultivated tobala? The overripening? The vats? Who knows, but when we talk about the future of mezcal, this is precisely the type of tradition that cannot disappear.

As for cultivated, semi-cultivated and wild agaves used to make mezcal, the bottom line is there needs to be awareness, planning and steps taken to be certain that all varietals of agave are sustainably available. Thankfully, many brands, producers, agave growers, restaurateurs, importers and others are highlighting these issues and taking action. The Pierde Almas and Wahaka reforestations are just two examples of what can be done to protect and manage this valuable resource.

But there is still only so much that can be controlled. If the entire community surrounding mezcal is on the same page, the likelihood of achieved sustainability would be very high. But this is not the case and cross-currents are everywhere. The growers may not be aligned with the producers. The producers may not be aligned with the brands (brands generally do not own their producers). The brands may be more focused on economics than preserving the traditions and sustainability of mezcal. So there are many factors that can screw the whole thing up, and the future is cloudy at best.

INTERNATIONAL SPIRIT COMPANIES AND MEZCAL

Mezcal, thankfully, is different from tequila on many levels. But specifically, it is not yet controlled by major corporations. And to produce a truly beautiful artisanal mezcal, it is difficult to foresee how one can be made in an industrialized setting. Among many processes, the roasting of the piñas in earthen pits clearly presents a scaling problem. But that may not stop the international spirit companies from getting involved.

In October 2013, Bacardi, one of the largest spirit companies in the world, signed a distribution deal with Zignum Mezcal. Here is an example of how things can potentially go wrong for mezcal.

Factually, Bacardi did not buy Zignum, they signed a deal to *distribute* Zignum. So while this was clearly not an acquisition of Zignum, many observers feel this will lead to an acquisition in the future. So who cares? I do. Everyone who drinks mezcal and shares a passion for it does, too. Why? Here is the core of the reasoning:

Industrialized mezcal at the Beneva facility.

1. Zignum is not an artisanal mezcal. It is made in a large industrial plant outside Oaxaca City with security guards, no photography allowed, and all that. Not an earthen pit in sight. It is nothing like the mezcal we have come to love. As it is promoted as a premium spirit, it is an affront to the mezcal culture in every way. Even tequila is embarrassed!
2. Bacardi will churn this industrial mezcal through its distribution channels and Zignum will produce more and more.
3. When Zignum produces more, they use more agave (though I am not sure it has actually been verified that they even use agave to make whatever this stuff is!). OK, it's agave.
4. Agave is a limited resource in Oaxaca and throughout Mexico. There is no annual crop. Eight years or so is about as quickly as agave can reach maturity and be harvested, but usually more like ten to twelve years is the minimum.

Am I unfairly picking on Zignum? It is not an artisanal mezcal. It does not taste like artisanal mezcal. It is not produced like artisanal mezcal. I have tried it, as have numerous people I know, and the consensus is that nothing in the spirit tastes like agave. Someone appropriately called it agavodka ("agave vodka").

Is this the future of mezcal? Even one such deal can negatively impact the mezcal world. When there is a limited resource and some relevant portion of it is being utilized sub-optimally, there is a problem. First, there is not enough agave to go around. Second, that puts upward price pressure on the agave

Top: I don't think this is happening at Zignum.
Bottom: Or this....

crop. While this may potentially benefit those who only grow agave, it doesn't benefit those who produce mezcal. Third, the mezcalero who buys agave for his beautiful mezcal may no longer be able to afford production. Finally, in the extreme, all agave (if there is any left) is used to make Zignum and Zignum becomes the future of mezcal. Ahhhhhhhhhhhhhhhh!!!!!!!!!! No, that won't happen. But directionally, I hope you see this is not a good way to go.

We all know mezcal is quickly gaining a foothold in the global spirits landscape, so it should be no surprise that the large international spirit companies—Bacardi, Diageo, Beam, etc.—are paying attention to this category. I know from the comments, traffic, emails and subscribers to my blog that the big guys are paying attention, and that is great! But if they want to get involved with mezcal, they should do it in a responsible way—a way that protects and respects the half-a-millennium heritage and culture of mezcal.

So Bacardi goes out and partners with a brand that makes an industrial mezcal. Bacardi may believe industrialized production techniques are the only methods able to produce mezcal in large volumes. Would it be challenging for an artisanal producer who today can produce 5,000 to 10,000 cases a year to get production to 50,000 cases annually? Yes, it will be challenging, but it can be done. At least a handful of brands with whom I've had this discussion believe they can do it. And more importantly, they believe it can be done in a *sustainable* fashion. Did Bacardi look into any of this? Do they know anything about mezcal? They have sizable tequila brands in their portfolio like Corzo and Cazadores, but do they know mezcal should not be produced like tequila? I don't know the answers, but I hope they are aware of these issues and have a plan that is not harmful to the environment or the broader industry. I can dream, can't I?

Is there anything positive that can come out of Bacardi's move with Zignum? Well, I guess I could argue it will raise awareness of the category, but there are risks as well. For example, I have a friend who vacationed in Mexico. While leaving, he made the required stop at Duty Free and bought a bottle of Zignum (I have forgiven him). After he bought it, but before he tried it, he asked me if it was any good. Not wanting to prejudice him, I told him I didn't know and he should tell me what he thinks. He soon reported back that it was nothing like the fine mezcals he had enjoyed with me on numerous occasions, saying something like: "It was bland. Not smoky and not very good." Yep. In his case, he knew mezcal was a wonderful spirit from prior experience. But what about the next guy who initially dips his toe in the mezcal waters with Zignum? He may be permanently damaged and beyond reeducation!

Maybe one good thing that can come out of Bacardi's move is an elevated dialogue and a new sense of urgency around the sustainability issue. The more brands, producers, consumers, bartenders, importers, distributors, academics, COMERCAM and even insignificant authors there are discussing this issue, the more likely it becomes for the industry to coalesce around this topic and develop solutions. So let's not be quiet. Bacardi and Zignum are just the tip of the agave.

ECONOMICS RULE THE DAY

There is a conundrum with sustainability pursuits: Agave growers and producers will not concentrate on sustainability efforts and plan for the long term until they know consistent demand will be there from the mezcal world. The tequila world has figured a lot of this out because they have consistent and growing demand for their product. Ultimately, all participants act in their own economic interests—that's the way the world works.

For example, from 2007-09 ethanol demand was soaring as was the price of corn. Many agave growers plowed over their agave fields to plant corn because they could turn a huge profit in less than a year. They did not know what agave prices would be five years hence when their crop matured, but they knew they could make a quick profit on corn today so they seized that opportunity. They have families to feed and have no romantic notions of mezcal.

A few things need to happen to break this mentality. First, producers need to own and grow their own agave, or have very tight alignment or contractual relationships with growers. Second, the producers have to know they have consistent demand from brand owners or from consumers if they are the brand owner themselves. Third, this means that mezcal needs to break out into the mainstream with consumers so there is consistent and growing demand all the way through the supply chain. This will incent planning and an enduring economic reality for producers and growers alike. It's obvious: To foster an environment of long-term planning and attractive economics for growers and producers we all need to do one simple thing—drink more mezcal!

Remember, the future of mezcal is not written. You and I and all of us have a hand in the future of mezcal. Maybe we play our cards by blogging, writing books or commenting on websites. Or maybe, as consumers, we simply vote with our wallets and support the brands that represent all that is great about mezcal.

By no means do I want to lead you to the conclusion that the future of mezcal is bleak. It is not, but it could be if all constituents ignore the implications of their actions. Mezcal is in full discovery mode by the world of bartenders, store owners, entrepreneurs, large companies, small companies and consumers. This ancient spirit is being enjoyed by more people than ever as they come to appreciate its heritage, culture, complexity, authenticity and smoky flavor. Continue to enjoy it and spread the word, just stay attuned to the fact that it is made from a limited resource that needs to be managed.

CHAPTER ELEVEN

Reading a Mezcal Label

The best mezcal is the one in front of you.

Mezcal labels are not consistent across the industry, with some labels providing a lot of information about the agaves, the producer, the region, etc., and some brands providing just a bit of detail. The more you drink mezcal, the more you want to learn and understand the differences between what each brand and producer have to offer.

Today, premium artisanal mezcals have reached a point where labeling has become "full disclosure," and I think it is fantastic. One of the things drawing people to mezcal is its authenticity, and the more you know about a product, the more real it becomes. Here are the details I like to see on a mezcal label:

- On the front of the label:
    - It starts with 100 percent agave. If that is not on the bottle, don't bother.
    - The type of agave. Again, not mandatory but highly preferred. Definitely becoming the way of the future.
    - Joven, Reposado or Anejo.
    - The percent of alcohol by volume (ABV).
    - Lot and bottle number. Not mandatory, but many put it on the label. It adds to the hand-crafted feel.
- On the back of the label:
    - Location of production and bottling. Sometimes just the distillery is listed.
    - Mezcalero, producer or distiller. These are all the same thing, but different brands use different terms. Again, not mandatory.
    - NOM number. For the product to be labeled as mezcal, the producer

MEZCAL
REAL
MINERO
Joven
100% Agave
Distilled
and bottled
in origin
since 1898
Double distillation
in clay pots
Alc/Vol 46.9%
Cont Net. 750ml
ESPADÍN, LARGO
TRIPÓN, BARRIL
Wild and cultivated Agaves
Bottle No. 146/906
Batch No. L-002
The Brand
Joven, Reposado or Anejo
100% Agave
Type of Still Used
The ABV
Type of Agave Used
Bottle Number &
Total Bottles in the Lot

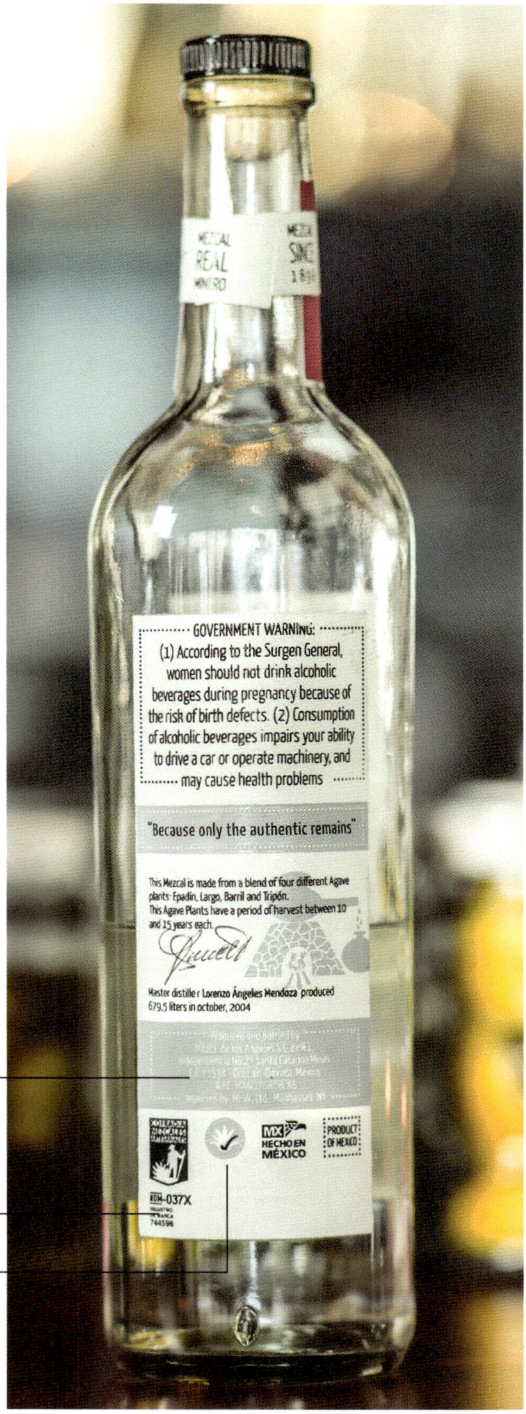

Where Produced & Bottled

NOM Number

COMERCAM Stamp

must be certified with COMERCAM and will have a NOM number. NOM is the acronym for Norma Oficial Mexicana (Official Mexican Standard). Most bottles have a NOM number and some also have a COMERCAM stamp. Some have both.

> COMERCAM stamp. Some bottles have it and some don't. But usually you have at least a COMERCAM stamp or a NOM number, sometimes both. If you see neither, be suspicious.
> Date of agave harvest, fermentation or bottling. You do not see this frequently, but it is becoming more common.
> Type of still used in production: clay or copper.

That tends to be the range of information you may see. What is on the front versus the back may be mixed and matched depending on the brand's preference. Let's see some of these items in action.

This Mezcal Real Minero bottle has a very complete label, and tells you everything you need to know and more. I particularly like the large clay pot on the front of the label as it is important and a real differentiating feature for the brand. Also, this joven is a blend of four different agave varietals—it is therefore an ensemble though they do not use that term to describe it.You see the NOM number is "O37X." The O and X are for Oaxaca, and they bracket the producer's certification number of 37. By comparison, I have a bottle of Mezcales de Leyenda, which is produced in Durango, and their NOM number is "D104G," where the D and G stand for Durango and they bracket the certification number of 104. So the NOM numbers will look slightly different depending on which of the eight certified regions produces the mezcal.

There clearly is a trend in mezcal labels to provide more information, and I doubt many would argue this is a bad trend. As I have said before, one of mezcal's great attributes is the authenticity of the spirit. It is not a spirit made in a nameless factory, by the production workers' local union, from a homogenous resource, in an anonymous town. Instead, mezcal is hand-crafted, on what are essentially small farms, by hard-working families, in remote villages, from specific agaves native to the local hillside. Authentic.

So putting all of this information on the label allows us to connect just a bit more to that mezcalero and appreciate the uniqueness and expertise which is poured into (and out of!) the producer's fine bottle of mezcal.

CHAPTER TWELVE

Traditional Versus Artisanal Mezcal

"If you want to keep your dignity intact, stay away from mezcal."

Alida Nugent (paraphrased)

As mezcal has grown in popularity in recent years, a debate has developed within the mezcal community concerning the differences, perceived or real, between a traditional mezcal and an artisanal one. I view the debate as unnecessary, high-minded and confusing to the current or potential mezcal drinker who hears this hoo-hockey!

While there may have been nuances of this discussion in Oaxaca for years, the most recent controversy began in the summer of 2012 at Tales of the Cocktail, a large spirits industry convention held in New Orleans. At this gathering, Pedro Jimenez Gurria, the founder of Mezonte, distributed a small pamphlet, *The Guide to Traditional Mezcal*. This guide was subsequently picked up by various news outlets, websites, etc., and ignited a bit of controversy. So who is Pedro, what is Mezonte, and why is his guide controversial?

Pedro is a deeply passionate mezcal aficionado who, in 2009, opened the first *mezcalería* in Guadalajara, Pare de Sufrir ("Stop Suffering"). Since then he has dedicated himself to promoting and defending traditional mezcal. In order to further spread knowledge of mezcal culture, Pedro opened a non-governmental organization with a mezcal tasting room called Mezonte. From Pedro:

> *Mezonte is an organization that we created to protect and spread information about traditional mezcales through tastings, videos, texts, academic, biological, cultural, gastronomica aspects, conversations, etc.*

Pedro's highly regarded bar Pare de Sufrir.

OK, got that. Mezonte is trying to be a positive force for mezcal, and in particular *traditional* mezcal, as they have defined it. But as soon as one starts defining traditional mezcal, particularly in a limiting fashion, it implies all other mezcals are not traditional, and this is a problem. I say "limiting fashion" because this is how Mezonte has defined traditional mezcal:

1. Look for "100 percent de agave" in the label.

2. Minimum alcohol content to be 45 percent (90 proof).

3. Label should indicate the exact provenance (village or state) of the mezcal, as well as the type of maguey used and the mezcal's craftsman, or maestro.

4. Shake the bottle to check for the formation of bubbles, or pearls. If no pearls form, do not buy the mezcal unless alcohol content is 55 percent or higher. You can also do this by pouring the mezcal from one glass to another.

5. If a mezcal shows an amber color, do not buy that mezcal. It's either rested (reposado) or aged (anejo) in wood or artificial coloring. In either cases the flavor and delicate aromas of the mezcal are destroyed.

6. Rub a drop of mezcal between your hands. As it evaporates you will be able to smell the aroma of cooked maguey. If it's a bad mezcal it would smell like alcohol or nothing at all.

7. Smell the mezcal before drinking it. You will find the aroma you sensed when rubbing it between your hands. Different aromas will soon become apparent. Keep your mouth closed as you initially breathe in the scent, and open it to fully recognize the aromas.
8. Take a small sip, rinsing your mouth with the mezcal for ten seconds, exhaling its vapor through your nose. Swallow the first sip and focus on the flavor coming to life on your palate. Do this a couple of times more and after several minutes your palate will be blossoming with the flavor of cooked maguey.

Mezonte says that this is not their list, per se, but the generally accepted criteria to describe traditional mezcal. You can see why some of this is controversial; the points on 45 percent ABV and aging in particular stand out. It is one thing to provide a limiting definition. It is another to make pejorative statements like, "If a mezcal shows an amber color, do not buy that mezcal" and "delicate aromas of the mezcal are destroyed." These are inflammatory statements. The list could simply state: "Traditional mezcals are not aged" and leave it there. I will come back to this, but further to these points, Pedro provided this additional information to me via a Facebook post:

"There are in a certain way 3 different kinds of mezcales...

1. **Industrial**, that are made by industrial technology such as autoclave, thousands of liters, with a chemical engineer instead of a maestro mezcalero, well, you know what I'm talking about.
2. **Artisanal.** That can be made by maestros mezcaleros and some traditional techniques but is made basically for selling, not for self-consumption, so their goal is more to make money (not that is something wrong about it if you do it responsibly) over the purity of the tradition.
3. **Traditional.** Those that keep doing it for hundreds of years with ripe agaves, without any conservatives, fertilizers, artificial colors, sweeteners, and other stuff. They only use underground ovens, natural fermentation (without any kind of accelerators), and discontinuous distillation. But most of all, they are made for the communities where they are produced and represent that, an identity of a whole community. Just as their language,

their traditional clothes, their rituals. These mezcales are another cultural aspect to these communities."

So the key difference between artisanal and traditional is one of commercial motivation and pursuits? One is made for the community and the other is not? I would suggest that most premium brands found in the U.S. are made as he describes in point No. 3. From these points, there is really no difference in the production methodology, just a difference in the motivations to make mezcal. The artisanal group is perhaps more commercially oriented while the traditional group is more community focused. That's fine, but why make this a point of emphasis when marketing mezcal? In my view, it is a distinction without a difference.

This non-distinction is further highlighted when traditional mezcal is sold outside the community. Doesn't selling it outside the community negate its traditional mezcal standing? If it is truly a traditional mezcal, then it would not be for sale in the U.S. or anywhere outside of the community. As soon as that mezcalero takes it out of the community and puts a price on it, doesn't that invalidate its traditional mezcal status? I feel this highlights the absurdity of the attempted distinctions.

I believe most people with a vested interest in quality mezcal want the history, tradition and production methods to be honored, utilized and maintained. This is what makes mezcal authentic, and we don't want that changed. So I think it's great that organizations like Mezonte exist to promote the culture of mezcal. I just believe they are creating unnecessary and artificial distinctions that may potentially hurt the very people they are trying to help.

Mezonte is not the only entity supporting this view of traditional mezcal. In Oaxaca, Mezcaloteca, the previously mentioned mezcal tasting room and library, lists essentially these same factors as to what makes a traditional mezcal. Mezcaloteca is a wonderful advocate for quality mezcals and a must see if you are in Oaxaca. Apparently, when I first broached this topic on my blog, they posted my picture at the airport—not in a good way. As mezcal is virtually a religion in Oaxaca, my comments were an affront to many. I simply wanted to highlight the unnecessary distinction of calling one thing traditional and another artisanal when they are really the same thing—it can only create unwanted confusion for the growing mezcal category. Rest assured, I too want to protect the 400-year-old process of making mezcal.

Whether it is artisanal or traditional mezcal production, this is the way it is done.

Top: The fire is started and the rocks are piled on top.
Bottom: Piñas are ready to be placed in the horno.

Top: Bagaso is layered on the rocks and then the piñas are placed.
Bottom: Putting on the last of the piñas.

Top: The piñas are covered with burlap or other fiber.
Bottom: The whole horno is buried under a foot or two of dirt and is now set to bake for days.

The low key sign at Mezcaloteca.

I have also seen very high-minded views of mezcal which suggest it should not be consumed in cocktails. The cocktail movement has been integral to mezcal's popularity, and that view is counter to the desire to grow the category, create jobs and income, and bring an overall economic benefit to the people of Mexico. So I simply don't get people with a stake in the mezcal game who espouse these views. If they don't want to make cocktails with mezcal, no problem. If they don't want to drink mezcal cocktails, no problem. But to tell others they should not consume mezcal this way is a bunch of B.S.

Of course, I love the tradition and culture of mezcal and protecting the old ways of the spirit. As discussed, a mezcalero doesn't use a flux capacitor to determine the ABV of his mezcal—he uses his eyes. And what if the producer adds water to soften the flavor profile for the export market (i.e. we sissy Gringos)? I say, who cares??!! The mezcal was still produced in a traditional way. The producer or brand owner simply wanted a more approachable mezcal as a taste preference, and did not compromise the 400-year-old production process to get it.

For those who scoff at this, I suggest they look at many practices in use today that did not exist even fifty or a hundred years ago, let alone 400 or

500 years ago. Today, virtually all mezcaleros store their finished mezcal in plastic before bottling. Plastic is cheap and effective as a storage mechanism, so of course they do. Or they may use pickup trucks to bring their piñas out of the fields, as they are more efficient than burros or wheelbarrows. Neither of these nor other modern initiatives invalidates the historical production process. So let's not be dogmatic as long as the mezcal is authentic and produced with integrity.

Typical mezcal plastic storage tank.

For me, the two key points of contention on the Mezonte list are the ABV and the "blasphemy" of barrel aging. Let's look at those two components.

ABV CONTENT

If a 40 percent ABV mezcal has been produced in an artisanal fashion—the same way as it has been for 400 years—and water is added at the end to achieve the desired flavor profile, does that alter the fact that it is a traditionally produced mezcal? I don't believe so. Let's take a look at some of the more common and popular brands on the market with respect to ABV:

- Del Maguey Vida: 42 percent
- Ilegal: All 40 percent
- Los Nahuales: All 42 percent
- Sombra: 45 percent

- Mezcales de Leyenda: 40 to 42 percent
- Fidencio: 40 to 44 percent
- Wahaka: 40 to 42 percent
- Scorpion: 40 percent
- Pierde Almas: 47 percent plus
- Los Amantes: 40 percent
- El Buho: 43 percent
- Montelobos: 43 percent

These are probably the brands that I see the most in bars, restaurants and liquor stores. They are almost all below 45 percent and for the most part, they are produced in a very traditional fashion. The people behind these brands are deeply passionate about mezcal and have a strong desire to maintain the rich history and culture of our beloved spirit. It makes no sense to say these mezcals are not traditional just because the ABV has been brought down as a brand preference.

Now to be fair, there are many other brands in the market that are north of 45 percent. They are excellent and artisanally made—brands like El Jolgorio, Pierde Almas, Mezcal Union, Koch, Siete Misterios, Real Minero and many more. This is great as far as I am concerned. There are mezcals for all palates. Which brings me to aged mezcals....

AGED MEZCALS

I have a full chapter dedicated to this, so I will make this quick, but wow, this topic amazes me. It blows my mind that some would claim a traditionally produced mezcal is not, in fact, a traditional mezcal because it has been aged in oak barrels. So the piñas are cooked in earthen pits, crushed by a tahona, fermented in oak vats with airborne yeasts, and then distilled in a clay pot, and voila! ... You have a traditional mezcal. What if a producer wants to bring a range of taste profiles to market and decides to age some of it in oak barrels for some number of months to create a reposado and an anejo? In this case let's also say the result is beautiful with great complexity and tastes of vanilla, cinnamon, chocolate and cooked agave. It is wonderful, but do you no longer have a traditional mezcal because you have chosen to age it in oak? To me, that would be one odd conclusion.

Clearly I feel aged mezcals fall comfortably into the theoretical traditional mezcal category. But setting aside technicalities and even the possibility that mezcals really have never been aged throughout history, I say "so what?" Let's assume aging is new to mezcal. All mezcal producers, brands, marketers and parties with a vested interest should be encouraging the growth of the category. Everyone should endeavor to attract new consumers to mezcal. We want the person who enjoys a nice, peaty, aged scotch like Laphroaig to give mezcal a try. Or the guy who enjoys Pyrat XO Reserve Rum. Or cognac. Or bourbon. Or whiskey. Many spirits have aged categories. Aged variations expand the category. It is really that simple.

Finally, on aging, I would simply suggest that you try a few aged mezcals yourself. There are a fair number of brilliant, artisanal, hand-crafted premium reposados and anejos on the market—Sacacuento, Ilegal, Los Nahaules, Los Amantes and Espiritu Lauro, to name a few. Try them. You will find that the aging adds depth and complexity while still maintaining the character of the mezcal.

A QUALITY MEZCAL

I feel the conversation should be about the makings of a quality mezcal, not the arbitrary subtleties of traditional versus artisanal mezcals.

As you will see, my list of what makes a quality mezcal is similar to the Mezonte list, taking out a few things and adding a few others.

WHAT MAKES A QUALITY MEZCAL?

1. Must be 100 percent agave. Yeah, buddy.
2. Must have an ABV consistent with the mezcal Norma (36 to 55 percent). Logical.
3. Preferably the label will contain the state of origin, type of agave plant and name of the maestro mezcalero, or mezcal master.
4. Aged mezcals add diversity and excitement to the category.

5. Piñas are roasted in the ground in earthen pits. Of course.
6. Piñas are crushed by hand or using a tahona.
7. Fermentation occurs in open-air vats with airborne yeast.
8. Distillation involves copper or clay pot stills.
9. Production is on a palenque, not in an industrialized setting.
10. Mezcal cocktails, while a relatively new method to consume mezcal, are awesome and integral to the newfound appreciation and discovery of mezcal.
11. Mezcal is brilliant, historical, cultural and fun. Don't take it too seriously.

Of course, my last two points have nothing to do with the production aspects of mezcal, but I think they are important to modern mezcal culture.

SUMMARY POINTS

I know the hearts of Mezonte, and others trying to protect the integrity and tradition of mezcal, are in the right place. I also believe the historic production process should be maintained, as we do not want to go down the path of industrialization for mezcal. That would ruin it.

On the other hand, I don't think people should be so rigid in their thinking as to be divisive to the mezcal category by proselytizing and defining a term like "traditional mezcal" in an absolutist fashion. I don't think anyone benefits.

If Mezonte and others feel their eight-point list is truly worth preservation, that's great. Let's just call it something that does not divide the category, create friction between authentic brands, and add unnecessary confusion to the developing consumer base. I think a term like "community mezcal" captures the spirit of the distinction. Then bartenders, brand owners, liquor store owners and all others could simply say that "typically community mezcals have a higher ABV content and are not aged." That is simple, clear and not prejudicial.

Of course, the best approach is simply to call everything mezcal and then talk about some of the defining characteristics of a quality mezcal. Brand

A mezcalero's pride—we certainly don't want to lose this.

owners and producers can readily talk about the factors that differentiate their products. The mezcal market is growing quickly, and the sooner the stakeholders get on the same page, the better for the category. We can honor, respect and be true to the traditional ways of mezcal. And we can assist the commercial growth of the category by allowing for a wide variety of ABV content and acknowledging that aging mezcal in barrels has a place in today's market, among other differentiating factors.

MEZCAL AÑEJO
Imported from Mexico
100% Espadin Agave
40% Alc by Vol (80 Proof) 750 ML
AC
AGAVE DE CORTES
Extra Aged Mezcal
3 Years in white oak barrels
45.4% ALC VOL
CONT NET 750 ml
MEZCAL
Los Nahuales.
AÑEJO 100% AGAVE ESPADIN
NOM-O14X
COLECCION PRIVADA
EZCAL REPOSADO
PRODUCED FOR
ILEGAL MEZCAL
Special Edition
OAXACA, MEXICO

CHAPTER THIRTEEN

Barrel Aging Mezcal

Drops of time ...

While barrel aging is widely accepted and praised in the tequila world, it is somewhat controversial and occasionally disparaged in the mezcal world. Some view aged mezcals as blasphemy and have their mezcal knickers tied up in a knot! To me, such limiting beliefs are counter to the potential growth of the mezcal category.

There is little consensus as to when tequila was first barrel aged, though some suggest it may have been as early as the beginning of the 1800s. Remember, tequila is mezcal, so technically aging mezcal has a lengthy history as well. Setting that aside, barrel aging of tequila became accepted practice in the mid-1900s, and today aged tequilas are celebrated and revered and claim a substantial premium in the market.

Why has mezcal been left behind when it comes to the practice of aging? Likely because mezcal has always been hyper-local. For centuries mezcal has been made in isolated villages far from population centers, while tequila was centered in the relatively more populated area of Jalisco. Due to the geographic remoteness of mezcal's production, the trends prevalent in tequila were unseen by the mezcal world.

So while mezcal aging happened to a limited extent throughout the 1900s, it clearly was not common, and importantly, was perceived as unnecessary by many in the mezcal world. Certainly wonderful, unaged artisanal mezcals can come from the hands of a master mezcalero. They are smoky, fruity, peppery and bursting with roasted agave, minerality or leafy greens. Mezcal purists suggest barrel aging masks much of the precious subtlety and intricacy of a mezcal. While there is room for that argument, I believe aging can enhance the sophistication of a mezcal while creating new branches of flavor.

Much has been written about the effects of barrel aging in other spirits, from whiskey to rum to cognac. In the 1800s, rum producers from the Caribbean knew rum shipped in barrels to New York always arrived better than when it had left. Similarly, whiskey makers from Kentucky and Tennessee found flavor enhancements by the time their products made it down the Mississippi River to New Orleans. So barrel aging was born more out of happenstance than design. But once discovered, spirit producers embraced the nuances and differentiation that aging could bring to their brands.

Of course, today the practice is in full swing. In tequila there are many examples. At the top of the price list would be Clase Azul Ultra, which is aged for five years in Spanish sherry wood casks, and can be purchased at the striking cost of about $1,500 a bottle! Wow. I once saw this on a cocktail list featured in an ultra-premium $400 margarita. I asked the bartender how many of those he had sold. His reply: "You'd be the first." No kidding.

There are many fantastic anejo or extra anejo offerings in the tequila world. It is true some of them are so deeply aged they are closer to fine cognac than tequila, as much of the agave personality has been overwhelmed by the barrel. Still, many of them are fabulous in their own right. But here is perhaps the crux of the argument against the aging of mezcals: The character of the agave and the artisanal mezcal production is lost. On the other hand, an experienced mezcalero can create a unique aged expression with barrel aging, broadening the consumer base for mezcal and expanding the offerings for certain mezcal drinkers. It does not have to be for everyone.

Barrel aging is a craft unto itself—more art than science, with fascinating depth and nuance. This is illuminated below in an excerpt from an *Atlantic Monthly* article, "The New Science of Old Whiskey," by Wayne Curtis:

> *In April 2006, a tornado struck Warehouse C at the Buffalo Trace Distillery in Frankfort, Kentucky. In the aftermath, the building looked like a diorama: Part of the roof and one wall had been artfully removed to reveal the 25,000 barrels stacked inside. Miraculously, not a single one of those barrels was damaged—proof, perhaps, of the Major League manager Leo Durocher's maxim: God watches over drunks and third basemen.*
>
> *Repairing the warehouse took several months, and during that time the barrels on the upper floors were exposed to rain, heat and sun. Mark Brown, Buffalo Trace's president and CEO, joked at the time that the distillery should sell the whiskey as "tornado-surviving bourbon."*

It turned out to be no joke. The barrels were opened about five years later (the liquor inside had then aged for nine to 11 years) and, says Brown, "the darnedest thing is, when we went to taste the whiskey, it was really good. I mean really good." The company decided to label the bourbon "tornado surviving," and aficionados—who also found it superior to the usual product—quickly snapped it up. One went so far as to write Buffalo Trace and ask whether it planned to make more. "Not deliberately," Brown replied.

So that small exposure period of a few months, within the total of roughly ten years of aging, changed the character of the bourbon. Pretty cool stuff. The article continues:

This barrel flavoring takes place in part because alcohol is a solvent that gradually breaks down elements in the wood over time. White oak in particular has an abundance of appealing flavors, including vanilla, nuts and coconut, as well as butterscotch notes from sugars in the wood, which are caramelized during charring.

Mezcal is usually aged in charred barrels. As economics are a major concern for many mezcal brands, they frequently will use old whiskey or bourbon barrels in addition to new American or French oak barrels. Barrel choices add to the complexities and subtleties of the aging process. Buffalo Trace, encouraged by their "tornado surviving" bourbon is digging deeper to find what other influences a particular barrel may have:

The company's most intriguing foray into barrel science has been the Single Oak Project. It was conceived, according to Brown, when a pair of curmudgeonly warehouse managers, Leonard Riddle and Ronnie Eddins, started needling each other during a meeting, with taunts of "my whiskey's better than your whiskey." Brown told them, essentially, to put up or shut up by aging a barrel of the same spirit and then comparing the resulting whiskeys.

But as they discussed the rules of engagement, Riddle and Eddins realized that they faced a more vexing problem: finding two identical barrels. The three dozen or so staves in any given barrel likely come from different trees (possibly even from different states), and by dumb luck one of the men might end up with a honey barrel. So Riddle and Eddins started compiling all the variables that might affect a barrel, and soon had listed dozens, ranging from the age and size of the oak used, to the latitude and elevation where it grew.

To test all their variables, they calculated, they would need to make about 3,000 barrels. So they narrowed down the list to what they believed was a more manageable number of salient qualities, including growth rings per inch, soil quality, and whether the oak grew on a north- or south-facing hillside. Then they set off into the Ozarks to select trees. They returned with 96 white-oak logs, which were then cut in half to test another persistent myth: that a barrel produced from the upper half of an oak tree makes better bourbon than one produced from the bottom half. The logs were cut and dried and assembled as 192 barrels, each representing a different set of variables. The barrels were filled with freshly distilled whiskey, and left to age for about eight years.

The bourbon was bottled (which stops the aging process), and for the past two and a half years Buffalo Trace has rolled out an experimental batch about every three months. Consumers are tipped off about releases via the company's Web site and are asked to give feedback; at least one informal tasting club has sprung up for this purpose. (Buffalo Trace is also analyzing the bourbon in-house.) The 11th release is due this month, and the remaining single-oak bourbons will be out within the next two years. "We've already seen reviews where people have said wheat [bourbon] with the top half of the tree is really good, and rye [bourbon] with the bottom half of the tree is really good," Brown says. "We're going to have to think about that."

Yes indeed, more art than science. To my knowledge, none of this is going on with tequila and certainly not with mezcal. By comparison, the aging process for agave spirits is rudimentary, which is OK, but this type of experimentation happening at Buffalo Trace certainly makes you think about the possibilities.

I need to share one more example which highlights the endless number of options. Jefferson Bourbon, a small batch purveyor of fine bourbons, recently launched its own experiment. Jack Bettridge from *Cigar Aficionado* captured the spirit of the endeavor:

The founder of Jefferson's (Trey Zoeller), a negotiant of Bourbons and ryes, was locked in late night discussion with friends when he advanced the idea that whiskey might also profit from the agitation that the motion of the ship affords. "Typically I don't follow through on drunk talk," he says with a wry grin. "But this time I did."

The idea was to store barrels on one of his companion's ships, a 120-foot Russian trawler that was getting on in years. Most of what Zoeller deals in has aged to some extent when he buys it, but in this case he barreled new-make whiskey and sent it off to sea, where it became quite the tourist, making six passages through the Panama Canal and crossing the equator. The Bourbon sloshed around for three-and-a-half years before coming back to Kentucky where it was further matured to bring its age to more than four years.

The result is a whiskey that is intensely colored and flavorful in light of its age. Zoeller lays that to two factors. The motion that the ship imparted on the casks (he likens it to a paint can in a shaker) certainly caused accelerated interaction with the wood. Zoeller adds that the temperature in the hold often topped 120° Fahrenheit as it sailed the tropics.

"It totally exceeded my expectations," says the producer. "It actually caramelized." He compares it to a dark rum, young but with a lot of composition. In fact, Zoeller thinks of the whiskey as having three separate influences: its birth in Kentucky, the temperature conditions enjoyed by a Caribbean rum, and the salt air atmosphere weathered by an Islay whisky.

Nahhhh … that doesn't sound interesting at all! I can imagine a fine artisanal mezcal joven, like El Jolgorio Arroqueño, sloshing around in a barrel on a cargo ship for a few months or more, breathing in the briny salt air, exposed to the tropical heat and sun on the deck, and arriving at its destination—my mouth! I know of few, if any, mezcal lovers who would not love to try something like that.

I have no idea if it would work, but that's not even the point. The point is barrel aging is *interesting and fascinating,* and the possibilities of what it can do to a mezcal are virtually endless. Further, as aging mellows and lessens the sharpness and smokiness of mezcal, the resulting flavor profile is appealing

Barrel aging of mezcal.

to a broader range of consumers. Also, people are accustomed to the joven, reposado and anejo range of tequilas so it's logical from a marketing perspective—it expands the market.

Interestingly, I have often heard mezcal ages more quickly than tequila. Mezcaleros perceive mezcal takes on the character of the wood more quickly.

I know of no scientific explanation for this, or even if it is true, but my personal experience suggests something different is going on. I know of precisely one brand, Scorpion, which deeply ages mezcal. Scorpion makes a five-year anejo and a seven-year anejo. Doug French, the producer, makes a fine mezcal but to me his extra anejos taste overly woody. I thought I was going to love them, but the barrel overpowers the character of the agave, so they simply don't work for my palate.

By contrast, a deeply aged tequila seems to get better and better. Certainly, the agave presence diminishes over time, but it trends toward a cognac and does not become overly woody in most cases. As the tequila aging process is far more advanced and industrialized, the aging frequently takes place in a more controlled environment, such as underground caverns. Whereas mezcal is typically aged on the palenque in a somewhat uncontrolled environment with barrels possibly exposed to the elements of weather, among other things.

Which brings us back to the thesis that mezcal ages more quickly than tequila. There is an interesting observation from the above *Atlantic Monthly* article which may have implications for mezcal aging:

> *It's long been known, for instance, that climate affects aging time. Rum and tequila are typically aged in the steamier West Indies or Mexico, which results in shorter aging times. Dave Pickerell, a former master distiller at Maker's Mark, told me about an experiment that took place some years ago when a barrel of bourbon was shipped to Scotland to age, and a barrel of scotch was shipped to Kentucky. The verdict? One year of aging in warmer Kentucky was the equivalent of about three or four years of aging in cooler Scotland.*

So if tequila is typically aged in cooler, controlled, underground chambers, and mezcal is typically aged in the open and more heated air of southern Mexico, that alone could explain why mezcal ages more quickly. Oaxaca is far hotter than an underground cavern, and surely a spirit would age more quickly there. This does not end the debate of whether mezcal *should* be aged, but it does highlight how the aging pattern might be different.

While I have found deeply aged mezcals a bad fit for my palate, mezcals aged in the range of several months to one year can be fantastic. A rough maximum of one year feels about right to me, though the sample set is small for anything beyond a year. Other than the above mentioned Scorpion, I am aware of only one other brand, Agave de Cortes (three-year extra anejo), that ages beyond one year. It is actually fantastic, but presses the envelope in terms of losing the agave character.

In the one-year aged anejo category, there are a number of excellent mezcals including Scorpion, Sacacuento, Agave de Cortes and Ilegal. The Ilegal Anejo holds a special place in my heart as it was one of the first of the new wave of premium mezcals which began to arrive in the late 2000s, and the first aged mezcal I had tasted. I thought it was brilliant then, and I think it is brilliant now. It is wonderfully smooth and gently smoky, with hints of caramel, vanilla and cinnamon, yet the character of the roasted agave is ever present. For anyone who believes mezcal should not be aged, try that one and come back to me! I accept your apology in advance.

And let us not forget about the reposados. A "repo" can be aged from a minimum of two months to a maximum of one year. While many mezcal drinkers enjoy an aged mezcal, some prefer a repo to an anejo because it is less refined and the agave more prominent. Here too, the number of labels producing repos is fairly limited compared to the number of brands in total (most brands do not offer aged mezcals). A few of the better repos I have tried include Los Nahuales, Los Amantes, Ilegal and Espiritu Lauro.

Remember, mezcal is supposed to be fun. Being high-minded about proper mezcal protocol with respect to barrel aging is so boring. The possibilities are endless and even though today mezcal producers are only scratching the surface on aging techniques, their products are already amazing. Plus, barrel-aged mezcals help expand the category to consumers who are otherwise not prepared to drink it.

For first-time mezcal drinkers, I always try to start them off with an aged mezcal, if handy, as an introduction to the spirit. Nine out of ten times, they love it. By contrast, when an aged mezcal is not available for a newbie, I pour a joven. Here the hit ratio is perhaps five out of ten who love mezcal on introduction. This is telling, and of course strengthens my belief that aging has a rightful place in mezcal production. Trust your palate, and I am sure you will agree.

CHAPTER FOURTEEN

Mezcal Will Change You

"A computer makes more mistakes faster than any other invention, with the possible exception of handguns and tequila."

Mitch Ratcliffe

As I have mentioned, I have had a long and passionate love affair with tequila. I have many gorgeous bottles of tequila around my apartment that are now simply gathering dust. Tequila has been a long-standing companion, but is being pushed aside.

But it is not just me. Tequila fans are dropping like flies all around me. At Anejo NYC in Hell's Kitchen, I had a holiday cocktail with my friend Chris who has been a tequila drinker for years, but had never really gotten into mezcal. This night, he ordered a mezcal margarita, and as I looked at him a bit surprised, he said, "Yeah. That's it. I don't think I'm going back." That's right. Suddenly, mezcal found him and he didn't think he could go back to tequila. Once you get used to the complexity of mezcal, tequila seems so ordinary. I used to worship tequila! Now it's just blah, blah, blah....

Sure, I still drink it and many are fantastic. But if mezcal is around, that's what I have. I had another recent exchange with my friend Mario, a long-standing tequila co-conspirator of mine. We have been talking about mezcal for years, and he just could not get there for some reason. Then we went to Cabo (not a mezcal mecca but we made it happen anyway) and searched out every bottle at every bar that we could find. We drank a lot of mezcal—some amazing, some good and some less so—but we tried what we could find. I think it was the silvestre mezcals—of which we drank copious amounts—that triggered the following email exchange between my buddy and me following this trip. He had just ordered a couple cases of mezcal:

Me: *Wow! Nicely done. I can recall a time not so long ago, like maybe 2 yrs, when you and mezcal were at a bit of a stand-off. It really just wasn't working for you, and look at you now! Shipping in cases at a time. But it is funny, right? For me, I rarely drink tequila anymore. Even the good stuff that I previously used to cherish. I just find it so BORING. So refined. So blah. I think it is starting to happen to you too. You think?*

Mario: *Yes, "it" is indeed happening to me now and you were a leading indicator in this case. Look at the results of my six bottle purchase last summer.....of 4 mezcals: Banhez, Koch and Siete finished! And of two tequilas: one barely opened and the other totally unopened!.....my consumption pattern speaks volumes......and admittedly, tequila isn't really interesting any more to me either.....*

This is what happens. Mezcal seems untamed compared to tequila and most other spirits. You get used to the unrefined and diverse nature of mezcal and suddenly everything else is blasé. The diversity comes from the wide variety of agaves and production methods that make no two mezcals alike. I'm not suggesting that all tequilas are alike, because there are significant variations between brands, production regions (lowlands versus highlands) and production methods. But with mezcal the range is much greater. Do you like Vince Vaughn? Me, too. He's hilarious. *Swingers, Wedding Crashers, Old School, Couples Retreat, The Break-up, Dodgeball* and so on—he basically plays the same role every time. I like him, but you don't get a lot of diversity. Now look at Jack Nicholson: *The Departed, Something's Gotta Give, The Shining, The Bucket List, A Few Good Men, Prizzi's Honor, Chinatown, One Flew Over The Cuckoo's Nest, Easy Rider, Terms of Endearment, As Good As It Gets, Ironweed, The Witches of Eastwick.* Need I continue? Vince, while I love him, is tequila—his range is limited. Jack, on the other hand, is mezcal.

Mezcal lovers understand every word I have just said. Tequila drinkers, if you are reading this book, your tequila collection is already in jeopardy of being ignored for the next thirty years or so. So be warned: Mezcal will change you.

CHAPTER FIFTEEN

Hosting a Mezcal Tasting

There are many books and websites that talk about how to host a spirits tasting. On my blog, I have described several tastings I have hosted largely to expose friends to the brilliance, complexity and diversity of mezcal. As mezcal offers such a wide range of styles and flavors, there are many ways to approach a tasting.

At the outset of your tasting, don't forget to show your guests this neat little parlor trick. Take a drop or two of mezcal and pour it into their palm. Tell them to rub it into their hands for a few seconds. Now have them cup their hands to their face and inhale. The smell is luscious roasted agave. If you are using cheap mezcal, this does not really work. But of course, if you are using cheap mezcal, you probably aren't reading this book!

For all of the below tastings, I would create note cards for each bottle with some basic information: the brand, varietal, ABV, aging, tasting notes and anything else you find relevant. Here a few ways to organize a tasting:

- **Favorite Bottles Tasting.** Simply line up your five or ten (or fifty in my case) favorite mezcals and compare and contrast. You may have jovens, repos, anejos, pechugas, silvestres and a few more so the comparisons are tricky, but you can still determine what you favor. In this type of tasting, I've found aged mezcals, if offered, usually prevail. They are more gentle and refined, so unless your crowd is a deep mezcal crowd, the repos and anejos will shine. Nothing wrong with this—they are amazing spirits.

  Sample: One night some years ago when my mezcal collection was in its infancy, I decided to hold a tasting for myself. My wife was out and my son was asleep, so I grabbed a few bottles as I wanted to see how they stacked up against each other. The lineup was: Del Maguey Vida, Pierde Almas Dobadaan, Mezcalero No. 2, Fidencio Sin Humo, Los Nahuales Reposado, Del Maguey Tobala and Ilegal Anejo. A bit of a

A silvestre table at one of my tastings.

random assortment, but all excellent. By comparison though, the Ilegal Anejo was my hands-down favorite that night. But this was a bit like the old Pepsi Challenge, where Coke was pitted against Pepsi. As Pepsi is sweeter by comparison, it usually won when tasted side by side. In this case Ilegal isn't sweeter, but much more subtle and less strident by comparison. It really was not a fair test as these mezcals are a fairly divergent group, but I had a great time!

- **Joven, Repo or Anejo Tasting.** You could hold three unique events featuring the three levels of aging. The repo and anejo categories are limited in terms of breadth of offerings, but they can be found. They are also pricey so assembling these tastings may stretch your budget. The jovens are the easiest way to go as your mezcal collection (or soon to be emerging mezcal collection) will probably be dominated by jovens.

  Sample: If you were to set up a reposado tasting you might include: Ilegal Repo, Los Nahuales Repo, Espiritu Lauro Repo, Los Amantes Repo, Agave de Cortes Repo and Don Amado Repo. Los Amantes Repo and Ilegal Repo are made by the same producer but taste completely different. You will enjoy the experience of contrasting these fine repos.

Also, within the same tasting, you could set up separate flights and have joven, repo and anejo tables. That will make for a lot of mezcals to taste, but no one is likely to complain!

- **Silvestre Tasting.** There are so many good wild agave bottles out there, and they deserve a special focus. Although you will likely have silvestres from different producers, this is still an excellent way to get a feel for the unique taste profile of an arroqueño versus a tepeztate, for example.

  Sample: You might include: Siete Misterios Arroqueño, Wahaka Tobala, Del Maguey Wild Tepeztate, El Jolgorio Barril and Pierde Almas Dobadaan.

- **Ensemble Tasting.** These are the blends and there are some great ones available. They include a wide range of agaves and taste profiles, though they are generally more closely grouped together than say the range found in a silvestre tasting. Also, you could combine a Silvestre Tasting with an Ensemble Tasting and contrast the single variety bottles with the ensembles.

  Sample: Koch El Mezcal, Mezcalero No. 4, El Silencio, Mezcal Vago Ensamble and Mezcal Unión.

So there are a few ways to host a tasting. You can really do it anyway you want as there is no right and wrong way to do this, as long as you have a good time. You also may want to pick a few specific bottles with which you are very familiar and describe to your guests what you taste and what they might look for.

At the outset, ask your guests to take a sip of the first bottle, hold it on their tongues, swish it around their mouths and then swallow. The first sip can be a shock to the system—full of smoke and heat—especially if you are new to mezcal. But the second sip will be completely different. Your palate will adjust, and once you get past the smoke, the rich complexity of roasted agave, citrus, spice, caramel, anise, floral, fruit, minerality or green vegetables will emerge.

You can make your tasting as formal as you want. Mine are more like a roving cocktail party. Also, don't forget to have plenty of sal de gusano and fresh orange slices so your guests can taste mezcal in the traditional Oaxacan way. But most of all, remember mezcal is fun, so don't take it too seriously!

CHAPTER SIXTEEN

Cocktail Time

Cocktails are a fantastic way to enjoy mezcal and have been integral to the spirit's invigoration in the U.S. and around the world. Yes, if I want maximum, full-on mezcal, I drink it neat. But that's not always the case for me, and certainly cocktails are an excellent introduction to mezcal's smoky allure. So I have put together a list of some of the finest and most diverse mezcal cocktails, while maintaining practicality. Many mezcal cocktail recipes are exceptional in taste but also call for exceptionally obscure ingredients—they are great, but too complicated for *this* home mixologist. While I have mostly avoided these recipes, I've included a few that take a bit more work because they are worth the effort. Also, some of these use unique liqueurs, vermouths or bitters. While you may not want to go out and buy every obscure ingredient (or maybe you do), it is worth picking up a few as they last a long time and the associated recipes are fabulous—plus one cocktail needs less than an ounce of these one-off additives.

These cocktails will amaze your friends and gain you newfound street cred. As you are pouring your first round of beautiful mezcal cocktails, don't forget to show them the neat parlor trick discussed in the tasting section.

A few tips before you begin:

1. **Always use fresh lime juice.** It makes all the difference in the world and there really is no substitute. I usually buy twenty or so limes at a time, squeeze them all and store the juice in baggies in the freezer. It is good for months. If you start getting serious about your mezcal cocktails, buy a real lime squeezer such as the Hamilton Beach 932 Commercial Citrus Juicer. It costs about $175 on Amazon and is worth every penny if you regularly make cocktails with fresh juice.

2. **Buy agave nectar** which can be found at most any grocery store. It is debatable whether it is healthier than sugar as a sweetener—some say yes, some say no. But I like the taste and it works well with mezcal and tequila. I use it instead of simple syrup in many of the recipes below.
3. **Try to garnish your cocktail with *something*.** It does not have to be a fancy fruit carving; usually a simple lime wedge will do. But it will visually bring your cocktail to life.
4. **Buy a Boston Shaker.** You know the large metal cups bartenders use? That's a Boston Shaker. You can get two metal cups or one metal cup and one pint glass. I like the metal and glass combo. The shakers most people buy with the cap do not work for me. All too often you cannot separate the pieces once it gets cold and it drives me nuts. A Boston Shaker is simple, effective and cheap, which is why every bar in America has one. Buy a little metal strainer to go with it.
5. **Buy a drink muddler.** You can find them at Bed, Bath & Beyond, among many places. It always comes in handy and is a great bar tool.
6. When the recipe says "mezcal joven," I suggest an espadin joven. Most of the jovens in the $35 to $50 range are espadin and are well suited for cocktails. You can use Ilegal, Wahaka, Fidencio, Del Maguey Vida or any other. Just don't use your $100 bottle of tobala!
7. To salt the rim of a glass, cut a small slice into the middle of a lime wedge and rub the lime around the rim of the glass. Dip the rim in salt (simply pouring salt onto a plate or into a small bowl works fine) and rotate to coat the rim. When you pour a cocktail into a glass with a salted rim, be careful not to fill the glass all the way to the rim as it will dissolve the salt on the interior of the glass and leave you with a very salty drink. I've seen many bartenders do this and it drives me nuts! Don't follow their bad lead.
8. For the recipes below, always put the ingredients in a shaker with ice unless otherwise specified. Not only does the ice make it cold, it also slightly dilutes the cocktail which has been accounted for in the recipe. Also, if the recipe calls for serving the drink on the rocks, use a rocks glass.
9. I have hosted many cocktail tastings over the years, collecting and discarding recipes, but always noting the best. With many of the recipes I have

included quotes from my fellow drinkers that add perspective to the cocktail and I have starred the recipes that are personal favorites.

The list below starts with the cocktails which are most easily made. From there, the complexity of creation may increase, but remember, they would not be included if they were not worth the effort. Now let's make some cocktails!

THE SIMPLE MEZCAL MARGARITA*

2.0 oz. mezcal joven
1.0 oz. agave nectar
1.5 oz. fresh lime juice
Splash of triple sec
Salt on the rim

"So simple and yet fantastic!" Put all the ingredients into a shaker and serve on the rocks with salt on the rim. Garnish with a lime wedge. Simple. Easy. Perfect.

Mezcal Margarita

SANTA DOMINGO

2.0 oz. mezcal joven
.5 oz. St-Germain
.5 oz. agave nectar
1.25 oz. lemon juice
Sal con gusano on half the rim

"A great cocktail for mezcal beginners." It cannot get simpler than this so when you are pinched for time, this works. Just load it all into a shaker with ice and serve on the rocks. Salt half the rim with sal de gusano. Garnish with a lime wedge.

POSSESSION*

1.0 oz. mezcal joven
1.0 oz. fresh lime juice
.75 oz. Luxardo Maraschino Liqueur
.5 oz. Green Chartreuse
Salt on half the rim
Luxardo Maraschino Cherries

This is a refreshing cocktail and a modern twist on a margarita. Simply add all ingredients into a shaker and serve on the rocks. Garnish with a skewered Luxardo Maraschino Cherry. They can be found on Amazon and these are no ordinary cocktail cherries—they are amazing.

SPEED OF DELIGHT

(from Mezon Tapas Bar in Danbury, CT)

2.0 oz. mezcal joven
.75 oz. St-Germain
.75 oz. Dolin Blanc
Splash of fresh lemon juice

Dolin Blanc is a sweet vermouth which is dry and citrusy and works well with mezcal. St-Germain seems to work well with everything. Load ingredients into a shaker and stir with ice for thirty to forty seconds. Strain and serve up in a martini glass.

MEZCAL MULE

1.5 oz. mezcal joven
1.0 oz. fresh lime juice
1.0 oz. ginger beer
.5 oz. agave nectar

This is a take on a traditional Moscow Mule which is made with vodka. Add the mezcal, fresh lime and agave nectar into a shaker. Pour over ice in a cocktail glass and then add the ginger beer. Stir with a bar spoon. Garnish with a lime wedge.

Speed of Delight

La Otra Palabra

MEZCAL FLOATER

1.5 oz. silver tequila (Herradura or equivalent—nothing cheap!)
.5 oz. mezcal joven floated on top
1.0 oz. agave nectar
1.5 oz. fresh lime juice
Salt the rim

For the margarita drinker who is just warming up to mezcal, this is another starter kit. Add the agave nectar, lime and tequila into a shaker and serve on the rocks. Garnish with a lime wedge.

LA OTRA PALABRA

("The Other Word," from L.A. bartender Eric Alperin)*

2.0 oz. mezcal joven
.25 oz. Yellow Chartreuse
1.0 oz. fresh lime juice
.25 oz. agave nectar
1 teaspoon Luxardo Maraschino liqueur
Luxardo Maraschino Cherries

Simple to make with fantastic results. Combine all ingredients in a shaker and serve on the rocks. Garnish with a Luxardo Cherry.

OAXACAN DREAM

2.0 oz. mezcal joven
1.0 oz. pineapple juice
.75 oz. cranberry juice
1.0 oz. fresh lime juice
.25 oz. agave nectar

This is a great introductory cocktail for new mezcal drinkers. Combine all ingredients in a shaker and serve on the rocks with ice. Garnish with a lime wedge.

EXIT MUSIC

*(from Liberty Bar in Seattle)**

1.5 oz. mezcal joven
.25 oz. Fernet Branca
.5 oz. prickly pear puree
.5 oz. fresh lemon juice
.25 oz. agave nectar
2 dashes lemon bitters

"Wow." "Different and amazing." If you have the ingredients, this is simple to put together. The prickly pear syrup is expensive and only found at specialty shops. Fernet Branca is a bitter aromatic spirit, so you probably want to keep it to a quarter of an ounce as specified. The sweetness of the puree and agave nectar balances the Fernet nicely and the citrus always works with mezcal. Put all ingredients into a shaker and serve on the rocks. Garnish with a lemon twist.

DEATH TO EL GUSANO

*(from Brandon Lloyd Burkart at Haddingtons in Austin, TX)**

2.0 oz. mezcal joven
.25 oz. St. Elizabeth's Allspice Dram
.5 oz. fresh lime juice
.25 oz. agave nectar

"The Allspice does something amazing to the drink." The St. Elizabeth's is a bit hard to find, but worth the effort—this cocktail is always a big hit. Combine all ingredients in a shaker and serve on the rocks with ice. Garnish with a lime wedge.

UNDER THE VOLCANO

*(from Los Americanos in NYC)**

1.5 oz. mezcal joven
1.0 oz. jalapeno/rosemary simple syrup
.75 oz. fresh lime juice
2 dashes teapot bitters
Sal con gusano on the rim

Under the Volcano

"Holy crap! This is incredible!" Everybody loves this cocktail—the simple syrup is the trick. To make the simple syrup, add ½ cup sugar, ½ cup water, two jalapenos split or quartered, strip a 4-inch length of fresh rosemary, and bring to a quick boil. Set it aside and let it sit for about twenty-four hours. The rosemary is there immediately, but it usually takes a while for the jalapeno to infuse. Strain after there is a bit of heat.

Combine all ingredients into a shaker and serve on the rocks. Watch the reaction.

Mexican Firing Squad

MEXICAN FIRING SQUAD*

2.0 oz. mezcal joven
.5 oz. Pomegranate molasses
.5 oz. agave nectar
1.5 oz. fresh lime juice
1.5 oz. sparkling water (optional)

This takes a bit of work to make the Pomegranate molasses, but it is worth the effort. Pour a bottle of Pom into a saucepan—the bigger the better as it reduces dramatically and you can store it for a long time in your fridge. Reduce it at a low boil and just when it starts to thicken a little bit, it is done. This will take anywhere from forty-five minutes to an hour and a half depending on the amount of Pom, size of saucepan, etc. Let it cool. Simply add all the ingredients above into a shaker and serve on the rocks. If you add the optional sparkling water, pour it into the glass after you have poured the drink, and stir with a bar spoon. Garnish with lime wedge.

SWEET LIPS*

2.0 oz. joven mezcal
.5 oz. vanilla simple syrup
1.0 oz. lemon juice
.25 oz. agave nectar
1-2 slices of serrano
Rim half the glass with sugar

To make the vanilla simple syrup, use ½ cup sugar and ½ cup water plus one vanilla bean. Split the vanilla bean along its vertical length and scrape out the black vanilla paste. Put all of this (bean and vanilla paste) in a saucepan with the sugar and water, then bring it to a quick boil to dissolve the sugar. Pour it into a jar and let it sit there for four hours or so—it can stay longer to magnify the vanilla flavor if you like. Next, strain it with a fine strainer. Specks of black vanilla paste will remain in the syrup but don't let that bother you. For the drink, muddle the serrano with lemon, add the syrup, mezcal and agave into a shaker and serve on the rocks. Rim half the glass with sugar. Garnish with a lemon twist.

LA PARKA

(from Gilbert Marquez, Los Angeles mixologist)

2.0 oz. mezcal joven
.75 oz. cilantro syrup
1.0 oz. fresh lime juice
2-3 dashes orange bitters
Rim the glass with chipotle salt

The cilantro syrup is a bit of a long way to travel, but worth the effort. And again, you can store in the freezer for months. Take one bunch cilantro, three cups of pineapple juice and one jalapeno, put them in a blender and puree. Strain the juice through a fine strainer. Now take that and mix with equal parts sugar in a saucepan and bring to a quick boil to melt the sugar. Let cool. Now you have cilantro syrup. Combine above ingredients in a shaker and serve on the rocks. To make the chipotle salt, simply take two parts salt and one part chipotle powder and combine. Yes, a lot of effort to make a cocktail, but it will blow you away. Garnish with a lime wedge.

FOUR AGAVE SAZERAC

(Casey Robison, Barrio Mexican Kitchen and Bar, Seattle)

.5 oz mezcal espadin
.5 oz mezcal tobala
.5 oz mezcal madrecuixe
.5 oz mezcal tequilana (blue weber)
2 dashes Peychaud's Bitters
2 dashes Angostura Bitters

Speaking of boozy cocktails, it does not get any boozier! Think of this as a create-your-own ensemble where you choose the brands. Put it all in a shaker with ice and stir for thirty seconds. Serve up in a martini glass and enjoy.

La Parka

Mezcal con Pepino

MEZCAL CON PEPINO

2.0 oz. mezcal joven
2.0 oz. fresh lime
.75 oz. agave nectar
2-3 slices of cucumber
2-3 slices of serrano pepper
Rim half of glass with crushed chili pequin and sugar

If you like spicy, this drink is for you. It is pretty simple except for the chili pequin and sugar rim, but it completes the drink. You can buy flakes of chili pequin at most grocery stores. Crush those flakes in a spice grinder so it is the same consistency of sugar. Once crushed, combine two parts sugar with one part chili pequin and rim half the glass. Put the serranos, cucumber and lime into your shaker and give them a good muddling. Add the agave nectar and mezcal into a shaker, and serve on the rocks. Garnish with a cilantro sprig. The cucumber adds balance to the pepper and the mezcal—this drink is brilliant!

DIVISION BELL

(adapted from Phil Ward at Mayahuel in NYC)

1.0 oz. mezcal joven
.75 oz. Aperol
.75 oz. Luxardo Maraschino liqueur
.75 oz. fresh lime juice

"Best in show." A universal favorite, which surprises me a bit because not everyone loves Aperol. It clearly works here. Combine all ingredients into a shaker and serve up in a martini glass with a grapefruit twist.

OAXACAN OLD-FASHIONED

(from Steve Olson, renowned spirits professional)

2 oz. mezcal anejo
1 bar spoonful of organic agave nectar
2 dashes Angostura Bitters
2 dashes Fees Gin Barrel Orange Bitters
Orange peel

"A very boozy and delicious cocktail." In a mixing glass put agave nectar, bitters and mezcal anejo, and give it a quick muddle or stir, then add large ice cubes and stir. Strain over fresh ice in a rocks glass. Express oils from a fat orange peel (1 inch wide by 2 inches long) over the drink and drop the peel in. You can play around and try different bitters, but some form of orange bitters should be in the mix.

THERE WILL BE BLOOD (ORANGE)

2.0 oz. mezcal joven
.25 oz. blood orange puree
1.5 oz. fresh lime juice
.5 oz. agave nectar

The blood orange puree is a tricky acquisition. You can buy it online or at specialty food stores like Kalustyan's in NYC. It is expensive, but you keep it in your freezer and it stays good forever I think. This is a great drink if you are having a party because the bottle of puree goes a long way. At any rate, mix all the ingredients in a shaker and serve on the rocks. Garnish with a lime. You can also substitute passion fruit puree for the blood orange and it too is yummy.

Oaxacan Old-Fashioned

THE MINTY MEZCAL

1.5 oz. Mezcal joven
.5 oz. fresh lime juice
1.0 oz. thinned agave nectar (same recipe as above)
4 cucumber slices
Strip leaves off 3 mint sprigs (3-4 inches long)

Muddle the lime, mint leaves, cucumber and agave. Add the mezcal and serve over ice in a rocks glass. Simple, easy and summer fresh! Garnish with a mint sprig.

LARKSPUR MEZCAL MARGARITA

(from Larkspur Restaurant in Vail, CO)

2 oz. mezcal joven
.5 oz. jalapeno simple syrup
.5 oz. thinned agave nectar
1 oz. fresh lime juice
3 cucumber slices
3 sprigs cilantro (2-3 inch stalks)
3 dashes Peychaud bitters

The only thing a bit time consuming is the jalapeno simple syrup. To do this, use simple syrup (equal parts water and sugar; for example one cup water and one cup sugar brought nearly to a boil to dissolve the sugar). Then, cut up one large jalapeno and plop it in. Let sit for one or two days (tasting regularly) and then strain out the jalapeno and seeds. You should taste it regularly during the infusing process to monitor the heat—you want it spicy but not overpowering. Keep it in the fridge and it is good for months.

To make "thinned agave nectar," just put equal parts agave nectar and water in a cup and heat in the microwave to homogenize the mixture. Heat and stir and it will be done.

With that, muddle the cilantro, cucumber, lime, agave and simple syrup. Add in the mezcal and bitters and put it all in a shaker. Serve on the rocks with or without salt on the rim. You will find the result to be magical. Garnish with a cilantro sprig.

BATTLE FOR PUEBLO

(apologies as I cannot recall where I picked this up!)

1.5 oz. mezcal joven
.5 oz. Royal Combier (triple sec will do in a pinch)
.25 oz. St-Germain
.25 oz. agave nectar
1.0 oz. fresh lime juice
¼ poblano pepper sliced and muddled

Half or quarter a poblano pepper, depending on the size, and muddle hard to release the juices. Add the other ingredients to a shaker and serve in a rocks glass. Garnish with a tall, thin strip of poblano standing in the glass.

MEZCALRITA

(from Mezon Tapas Bar in Danbury, CT)

1 oz. mezcal joven
.5 oz. Liquor 43 (a.k.a. Cuarenta y Tres)
1.5 oz. Honey Lemon Syrup (2 oz. honey, 2 oz. hot water, 2 oz. fresh lemon juice)
Sea salt on half the rim

"Delicious." "Women will like it." The honey-lemon syrup would probably make any cocktail taste amazing, and it works well here. (Note: You are making 6 ounces of syrup but only using 1.5 ounces per drink). Combine ingredients into a shaker and serve on the rocks.

EES BERRY BERRY GOOD

2.0 oz. mezcal reposado
2.0 oz. fresh lime juice
.5 oz. agave nectar
.5 oz. vanilla simple syrup
5 blueberries
2 raspberries

This is a great summer cocktail. Put the vanilla simple syrup (recipe in the Sweet Lips cocktail), blueberries and raspberries in a shaker and quickly muddle. Add the rest and serve on the rocks. Drop a blueberry in the glass for garnish.

Mezcal Martini

MEZCAL MARTINI

2.5 oz. mezcal reposado
1.5 oz. fresh lime juice
1.5 oz. agave nectar
Salt on the rim

This is another twist on a mezcal margarita. The repo adds something special and it could not be simpler to make. Mix all ingredients in a shaker and serve in a chilled martini glass. Garnish with a slim lime wheel floating on top.

MEZCAL NEGRONI

(Jay Silverman, Agave Restaurant NYC)

1.5 oz. mezcal joven
.75 oz. Campari
.75 oz. Carpano Antica
Thick orange peel slice

This is a mezcal twist on a classic negroni. Add the ingredients into a shaker and stir. Serve on the rocks. Express thick slice of orange peel over the drink and drop into glass.

Mezcal Negroni

Cilantro Bravo

MOM'S MEZCAL MARGARITA

2.0 oz. mezcal joven
.5 oz. brandy
2.0 oz. fresh lime juice
1.0 oz. agave nectar
3 dashes Peychaud's Bitters
Salt on the rim

Yes, my mother loves this version with brandy so it goes in the book—and I agree, it is pretty damn good. Add all ingredients in a shaker and serve up in a chilled martini glass or on the rocks. Garnish with a lime wedge.

SMOKY BANDIT*

2.0 oz. mezcal joven
.75 oz. Orange Curacao
.75 oz. pineapple juice
.5 oz. fresh lime juice
.25 oz. agave nectar
2 thin slices of serrano pepper

Add the lime and the serrano slices to a shaker and muddle the pepper to extract the juices. Combine the rest of the ingredients and serve on the rocks. Garnish with a slice of serrano floating on top.

CILANTRO BRAVO

2.0 oz. mezcal joven
2.0 oz. fresh lime juice
1.0 oz. agave nectar
4 sprigs cilantro

Aggressively muddle the cilantro in a shaker with the lime juice. Add the rest of the ingredients to the shaker and serve on the rocks. Garnish with a cilantro sprig.

THE LULU

*(from NYC bartender Lulu Martinez)**

2.0 oz. mezcal anejo
.75 oz. jalapeno simple syrup
1.0 oz. fresh lime juice
.5 oz. passion fruit puree
1 strawberry
1 raspberry
1 blackberry

Believe me, I hate to put something as beautiful—and expensive—as Ilegal Anejo into a cocktail, but this drink is so good it is worth it. You can always substitute a mezcal joven if you like and the drink is still great. Place the fruit with the lime juice into a shaker and give it a quick muddle. Add the other ingredients (simple syrup recipe is in the Larkspur Margarita) into the shaker and serve on the rocks. Garnish with a strawberry slice on the rim.

EL CONDE DE SAN DIONISIO

(from Florian Minier at Haddingtons in Austin, TX)

1.5 oz. mezcal joven
1.0 oz. Dolin Blanc
.5 oz. Yellow Chartreuse
1 dash celery bitters

"Not for rookies." It is a "boozy" cocktail. The bitters are great but keep it to a dash as it is a strong ingredient.

NAKED AND FAMOUS

(from Joaquin Simo at Pouring Ribbons, NYC)

.75 oz. mezcal joven
.75 oz. Yellow Chartreuse
.75 oz. Aperol
.75 oz. fresh lime juice

Combine all ingredients in shaker and serve up in a martini glass. Garnish with a lemon twist.

The Lulu

EL EMBARCADERO

(from The Bar Downstairs at Andaz Hotel NYC)

2.0 oz. silver tequila
.5 oz. mezcal joven
.75 oz. Carpano Antica
.75 oz. fresh lemon juice
1.0 oz. pineapple juice
.75 oz. agave nectar
Large grapefruit peel

"Very well-balanced and delicious." Combine all ingredients into a shaker and serve on the rocks. Express grapefruit peel over the drink and drop down the side of the glass for garnish.

KIWI MARGARITA

(from Dale Degroff)

2.0 oz. mezcal joven
.5 oz. Cointreau
.75 oz. fresh lime juice
.5 oz. agave nectar
½ kiwi (scoop out of the skin)

Dale Degroff, "King Cocktail," is never wrong. Muddle kiwi in a shaker until thoroughly crushed. Combine the ingredients in a shaker, strain and serve on the rocks. Garnish with a lime wedge.

THE MISFIT

(from Misfit Restaurant in Santa Monica, CA)

2.0 oz. mezcal joven
.75 oz. fresh lemon juice
.5 oz. honey syrup
Tiny splash of Yellow Chartreuse
1 slice of serrano

The honey simple syrup is equal parts water and honey. Muddle the serrano and then add the rest of the ingredients into a shaker. Serve up in a martini glass. Garnish with a lemon twist.

MAXIMILLIAN AFFAIR

(from Misty Kalkofen at Drink Boston)

1.0 oz. mezcal joven
1.0 oz. St-Germain
.5 oz. Punt e Mes
.25 oz. fresh lemon juice
Lemon twist

Combine all ingredients in a shaker and serve on the rocks with a lemon twist. This is a great cocktail—do not let the brevity of this description make you think differently! (Note: Punt e Mes is an Italian vermouth brand that is about half way between a sweet vermouth and Campari).

SIMPLEMENTE DELICIOSO

(from Liberty Bar in Seattle)

1.5 oz. mezcal joven
.25 oz. Campari
.5 oz. Cointreau
.5 oz. fresh lemon juice
.25 oz. simple syrup
2 dashes Peychaud's Bitters

"The mezcal shines through nicely, but does not overpower the drink." This cocktail is always well received. Combine all ingredients in a shaker and serve on the rocks. Garnish with a lemon twist.

THE OLIVIA

(from Max Kestenbaum at Del Monte Speakeasy in Venice, CA)

2.0 oz. mezcal joven
.5 oz. Domaine De Canton
1.0 oz. fresh lime juice
.5 oz. honey syrup
1 slice of cucumber

"A great summer cocktail." Muddle the cucumber then combine all ingredients in a shaker and serve on the rocks. Garnish with a lime wedge.

POBLANO ESCOBAR

(from Julian Cox at Rivera in Los Angeles)

2.0 oz. mezcal joven
.75 oz. Royal Combier
1.0 oz. fresh lime juice
Splash agave nectar
4 chunks fresh pineapple
2 or 3 small rings of poblano pepper (about ¼-inch thick)

Muddle poblano with lime juice and Royal Combier. Add pineapple, cumin and agave and muddle again. Add mezcal and serve on the rocks. Garnish with a slice of poblano.

THE WHOA MAMA

(from the Backyard Bartender)

1.5 oz. mezcal joven
.5 oz. Pom molasses
1.0 oz. fresh lime juice
1.5 oz. Ginger beer

Make the Pom molasses as described in the Mexican Firing Squad. Combine the lime juice, mezcal and molasses into a shaker. Add the ginger beer after you serve on the rocks and stir with a bar spoon. Garnish with a lime wedge.

MEZCAL BLOODY MARY

2.0 oz. mezcal joven
5.0 oz. tomato juice
1.0 oz. fresh lime juice
2 teaspoons Worcestershire Sauce
Ground pepper
Salted rim

Combine the mezcal, tomato juice, lime, and Worcestershire in a shaker. Serve on the rocks in a tall glass with fresh ground pepper floating on top. Garnish with a celery stick.

COLECCION PRIVADA
OAXACA, MEXICO
WAHAKA
100% Agave
Mezcal Vago
Arroqueño en Barro
Agave
Mezcalero
Village
Grind
Type of Still
Distillations
Batch Size
Fermentation Date
Age
100% AGAVE
APEROL

CHAPTER SEVENTEEN

Mezcal Brands Found in the U.S.

For everything bad, mezcal. For everything good, mezcal.

As we have discussed, mezcal sales are growing quickly and there should be no surprise that the number of brands being created, or being imported for the first time, is rising rapidly. So while it is a moving target, I try to stay up-to-date on the brands found in the U.S.

I have scoured the Internet, liquor stores, blogs, bars and restaurants in every city and every town in America to find any and every brand of mezcal that can be acquired in the U.S. OK, a bit of an exaggeration on the cities and towns, but other than that some serious scouring has been going on. Some brands are incredibly obscure and can only be found online at one or two places. Others are seen regularly at cocktail bars, liquor stores and high-end restaurants.

So here are the brands found in the U.S. as of January 2014. They are listed roughly in the order of their market presence, which means: They are in bars and liquor stores, can be found readily online and are actively promoted through Facebook, Twitter and other means. You likely see and often hear about the first ten brands on the list. The next ten or so have market presence, but to a lesser extent. After about the first twenty brands, it falls off sharply. Still, in the twenty-to-forty range there are some incredible mezcals, but they are just not widely known.

The bottom third of the list has some mass-market brands and others that are virtually impossible to track down, though I have seen them available online which is how they made the list. But I am not sure why some of these guys bother with the U.S. as they are almost nonexistent, have no website, and apparently make no effort to change that.

In summary, if you look REALLY hard you can find approximately seventy brands in the U.S. By contrast, tequila has more than 1,000 brands found in America, so mezcal has a long way to go.

I keep this list up to date on my blog, so you can always check there to see what is new. For now, this is what I know.

THE BRANDS

1. **Del Maguey.** They probably have the most significant market presence and are the pioneer of the premium mezcal category. Founder Ron Cooper started bringing his "single village mezcals" into the U.S. in the late 1990s. They work with many different producers, many different villages, and produce many different expressions and varietals. They have eight joven expressions under the "single village" umbrella, all espadins except for a tobala and a pechuga. And they have another eight very small-release bottlings under the Vino de Mezcal series, with several silvestre agaves including an arroqueño and tepeztate. They also have a cocktail-oriented, lower-priced version called Vida. Many to choose from, but you can never go wrong ordering a Del Maguey mezcal.

2. **Ilegal Mezcal.** One of the first in the wave of "new premium" mezcals to arrive around 2010 with a joven, reposado and anejo—all three espadin. The joven, by design, is less smoky than many mezcals and therefore more approachable. The reposado is luscious

DEL MAGUEY
SINGLE VILLAGE MEZCAL™
Pechuga
SANTA CATARINA MINAS

with vanilla and cinnamon, and the anejo is a transformative spirit. Called "Ilegal" as a nod to the brand's roots, as it was born smuggling mezcal out of Mexico to founder John Rexer's bar in Guatemala. Ilegal is beautifully packaged with a tequila formula of joven, repo and anejo.

3. **Fidencio**. Also a "new premium" arrival around 2010. This brand caught my attention early as they started with a *sin humo* (without smoke) expression, which I thought was an excellent way to introduce people to this new category of mezcal. As the market has evolved, Fidencio now has a smoky Clasico and a pechuga and does occasional varietals including a madrecuixe—all good stuff.

4. **Sombra**. Founded by wine sommelier Richard Betts (he now has a tequila, too), Sombra has one joven expression which is fairly smoky. While the packaging does nothing for me, the product is good, but perhaps a bit intense for a mezcal newbie.

5. **Pierde Almas.** Lovely mezcals with a number of varietals including espadin, dobadaan, tobasiche, tobala, tequilana weber, "+9" (a funky gin-like expression), regular pechuga and *conejo* pechuga.

The conejo pechuga is particularly interesting as it is made with a wild rabbit breast. Pierde also has a cocktail-oriented version called La Puritita. Clearly a very creative brand bringing a host of unique offerings and they are all excellent, although they lost my friend Mario at the tobasiche.

6. **Los Nahaules.** From Los Danzantes distillery, Los Nahaules brings a joven, a repo and an anejo. The aged versions are unique with a bit of an infused spice flavor—think nutmeg. All fine mezcals.
7. **Wahaka Mezcal.** With a fun play on the name Oaxaca, Wahaka produces an espadin, tobala, madrecuixe, ensemble and a reposado con gusano (ugh). They put the worm in their reposado as they feel there is a traditional element to these types of infusions. I might not drink this one but I love all the rest. They also get you really fucked up when you visit their palenque.
8. **Mezcales de Leyenda.** They produce three different jovens from three regions: Durango, *A. durangensis*; Guerrero, *A. cupreata*; and Oaxaca, *A. espadin*. The cupreata in particular is a break from the norm with a polarizing, musty taste. The durangensis is a bit challenging and not my favorite. The espadin is right down the middle and excellent. They also produce a cocktail-oriented version called el Peleton de la Muerta.
9. **Mezcal Vago.** A 2013 newcomer that has impressed with great mezcals and quick market traction. They have a tobala, espadin, cuixe, mexicano, ensemble and *elote*. The elote (translated as "roasted corn") is one of a kind where roasted corn is put into the still before a third distillation. They say the mezcal has subtle roasted corn notes with a gentle sweetness on the finish. I cannot quite find the corn flavor, but all of their mezcals are beautiful.
10. **Alipus.** From the prolific Los Danzantes distillery, Alipus offers four distinct espadin jovens from different producers: San Andreas, San Juan del Rio, San Baltazar Guelavila and Santa Ana del Rio. My friends at the Mezcalistas blog favor the San Andreas and I agree. The Santa Ana del Rio (on one tasting) was reminiscent of burned rubber and petrol—not my favorite and luckily can't be found nearly as easily as the other three.
11. **Montelobos.** Agave academic Ivan Saldana Oyarzabal teamed with fifth-generation mezcalero Don Abel Lopez to bring this mezcal to market in

2013 with unspecified backing from spirit giant William Grant. It is a well-balanced espadin which is sure to please.

12. **Los Amantes Mezcal**. They offer joven, reposado, anejo and silvestre (new to the market) expressions. As Los Amantes triple distills, the resulting mezcal is quite mellow and makes for easy drinking. The brand owner is also behind Casa Mezcal in NYC, an excellent restaurant and bar which is a shrine to all things mezcal.

13. **Scorpion Mezcal.** Founder Doug French uses aboveground ovens that give his mezcal a tequila-like gentleness. There is a silver, a repo, several anejos (aged one, five and seven years), tobala silver and tobala anejo, which is the only one in existence. He also is involved with three other brands, so Doug is a busy guy. Scorpion is notable for the scorpion found in every bottle—it is edible and tasteless (in more ways than one)—but overall these are quality mezcals.

14. **El Buho.** With passionate owner John Henry behind it, El Buho made its debut in 2012. Only an espadin joven is offered.

15. **Mezcalero.** Los Danzantes distillery works with tiny and remote producers to bring periodic releases where each batch is different from the last. A new release is rolled out every six months or so, and each is an ensemble of wild agaves. These are extremely limited releases and once they are gone, that's it. Releases No. 2 (only 620 bottles!) and No. 4 are my favorites so far, and they are up to No. 8 now. Drink 'em when you see 'em as they are all fantastic.

16. **Marca Negra Mezcal**. With a funky green bottle that has a black handprint on it, Marca Negra offers an espadin and a tobala, both jovens.

17. **Don Amado.** Unlike most of the brands on this list, Don Amado has been around for more than a handful of years—since 1994. They offer a joven, repo and anejo.

18. **Mezcal Union**. Class of 2012, this espadin and cirial blend was started by a group of Mexican entrepreneurs to bring their beloved spirit to the U.S. Joven only.

19. **Siete Misterios.** Again, they have many silvestre varietals available in Mexico, but only their top-of-the-bell-curve arroqueño can be found in

100% AGAVE MADRECUIXE SILVESTRE
FIDENCIO
MADRECUIXE
MEZCAL
DOUBLE DISTILLED BATCH PROOF
49.4% ALC BY VOL
JOVEN
100% Agave
Vago
GUERRERO
USDA
ORGANIC
750 ml
MEZCAL
Siete Misterios
ARROQUEÑO
MEZCAL JOVEN
100% Agave
ARROQUEÑO
2008

47% Alc/Vol
KOCH EL
MEZCAL
WILD AGAVE
100% AGAVE
750ML
MEZCAL
El Silencio
HECHO EN MEXICO
PROOF 80
100% AGAVE

the U.S. I hear they may be working with a new producer so the future of my beloved arroqueño is uncertain. Buy it if you find it.

20. **El Jolgorio**. Until recently, only their pechuga was available in the U.S. But now their tepeztate and others are available including an arroqueño, barril, cuixe and tobala, among others. They are expensive but fantastic. They also have a cocktail-oriented version called Nuestro Soledad.

21. **Real Minero Mezcal**. Their only U.S. offering is a beautiful ensemble of espadin, tripon, barril and largo. They have many more varietals available in Mexico from renowned mezcalero Graciela Angeles Carreño.

22. **Banhez.** Another Class of 2012 arrival, this is an attractively priced single expression barril joven.

23. **Koch el Mezcal.** One more attractively priced ensemble joven, it is made with wild agaves tobala, de lumbre, tobasiche and cirial.

24. **El Tieneblo.** Offering a joven, repo and anejo.

25. **Mezcal Yuu Baal.** While they have more expressions available in Mexico, only their madrecuixe joven can be found in the U.S. While the madrecuixe is quite good, I tried the reposado in Oaxaca and it tasted artificial and was the color of root beer.

26. **La Nina del Mezcal.** Passionate mezcal entrepreneur Cecilia Rios Murietta started this brand in 2012. To date, it can really only be found online or on the West Coast. Espadin joven only.

27. **El Silencio.** Launched in 2013 by Mexican entrepreneur Fausto Zapata, El Silencio is an elegantly packaged ensemble joven. Fausto told me that the label does not list the varietals as a means to stoke your curiosity about the brand. I told him I was closer to annoyed than curious, but his mezcal is excellent.

28. **Alacran Mezcal**. This is a mezcal produced in a non-smoky tequila style. Espadin joven only.

29. **Espiritu Lauro.** Infrequently seen but quite a nice espadin joven and reposado. Rumor has it that an anejo is coming in 2014.

30. **Delirio Mezcal**. Relatively new to the U.S., they have a beautifully packaged joven, repo and anejo. Only found on the West Coast and online at this time.

31. **Agave de Cortes.** The Cortes family is behind the El Jolgorio line as well. They have a joven, repo, repo con gusano (ugh!), anejo and three-year aged anejo. While I cannot figure why such a fine brand puts a worm in one of its bottles, I will say their three-year anejo is like a rich caramel and vanilla fueled cognac.
32. **Mezcal Tosba.** Arrived in the U.S. in mid-2013. Nice packaging with an espadin, tobala and pechuga.
33. **El Sacrificio.** Arrived in the U.S. in early 2014. Joven and gently aged reposado.
34. **Semilerro.** Not readily found but they have espadin joven, repo and anejo.
35. **Joya Mezcal**. Gran Reserva only and fairly underwhelming at that.
36. **Santa Pedrera.** Espadin joven only. Barely a website.
37. **Real Matlatl.** Fairly new to the U.S. with espadin joven, repo and anejo.
38. **Metl.** Imported since 2005, they have a joven and a repo.
39. **Dona Sarita.** Little information can be found. Joven espadin only.
40. **Cha Cha Cha Mezcal**. Arrived in the U.S. in late 2013. Only espadin joven is available in the U.S.
41. **Mezcal Embajador.** This brand has been around a long time in Mexico. In the U.S. they offer a joven, repo, anejo and Gran Reserva.
42. **El Zacatecano.** This is a tequila-like joven backed by former baseball star Edgar Martinez.
43. **Sacacuento.** Espadin silver and anejo only. The anejo is top shelf, but the brand is only found on the West Coast or online.
44. **Shawi.** Inexpensively priced with a strong anise flavor. This is another in the class of 2012.
45. **La Fogata.** Anejo only. Hard to find and not really worth the effort or the cost.
46. **Wild Shot**. Country music star Toby Keith is behind this brand, and he probably sells a fair amount of it through his chain of restaurants. Unfortunately, the mezcal is not great and it is derived from the still unknown species "Green Agave."

PREMIUM
HAND CRAFTED
100% AGAVE
MEZCAL
DE OAXACA
Don
Amado
NOM-0129X
RÚSTICO
Product of México
EL BUHO
MEZCAL

SnANDRES
MEZCAL
MEZCAL
MEZCAL
JOVEN 100% AGAVE
PRODUCT OF MEXICO
GUERRERO
USDA
ORGANIC
Net.Cont. 750 ml
2013
001- ARQ
300
MEZCAL JOVEN
THE WILD
MOUNTAIN
MAGUEY

Mezcal Vago
Arroqueño en Barro
100% Agave
Agave
Mezcalero
Village
Grind
Type of Still
Distillations
Batch Size
Fermentation Date
Age
WAHAKA
JOVEN ESPADÍN
47% Alc/Vol
COLECCION PRIVADA
OAXACA, MEXICO
100% AGAVE
MEZCAL
EZCAL JOVEN

47. **Monte Alban.** Most certainly the highest volume mezcal in the U.S. Also, most certainly not the best mezcal in the U.S. If you are desperate and dying for a mezcal, and it's all that can be found, have a vodka instead.

48. **Beneva.** Maker of Monte Alban and they also have their own brand. See above.

49. **Zignum.** You will see Zignum discussed elsewhere in this book. It is an industrial style, tequila-like tasting mezcal, and is not made in the traditional way. They have a joven, repo and anejo and signed a distribution deal with Bacardi in the fall of 2013. Many are concerned Bacardi will drive volumes to a level which stresses the limited resource agave.

50. **Maria Mezcal.** Joven, joven con gusano, repo and anejo.

51. **Mijes.** Imported by the Scorpion team. Joven and repo.

52. **El Senorio.** Same producer as Zignum. Their expressions are: Young with Two Worms, Aged with Worm, and Aged Extra. Eloquent.

53. **Oro de Oaxaca.** Imported by Doug French of Scorpion. Joven. I happened upon a bottle of this at a restaurant deep in the Patagonia region of Argentina. At first, I couldn't believe my luck as mezcal and Argentina don't mix. Then after trying it, I couldn't believe my *bad* luck. This stuff is truly awful—even Patagonia couldn't make it taste better.

54. **Herencia del Mezcalero**. Joven, repo, anejo and citrus.

55. **Mina Real.** This is Don Amado's entry-level brand produced in aboveground ovens. Joven and repo.

56. **Enmascarado Mezcal.** Found at one liquor store in L.A. Joven and turbo joven (54 percent ABV).

The rest of these barely deserve a mention. But this list covers all mezcals that can be found in the U.S., and these can be found—usually with great effort—although you probably would not be impressed with the results.

57. **Benesin.** Espadin and tobala offerings, joven only. Having tried them both, I would spend my money more wisely next time.

58. **La Penca Mezcal**. Joven with two worms. Can you guess my opinion on this one?

59. **Mezcal Felino.** No website or anything else. Joven.

60. **El Mal Pais**. No website.

61. **Mezcal Rojas.** No website.

62. **Mezcal Guerrero.** No website.

63. **Casa Curiel Mezcal.** No website.

64. **Aztecali Mezcal.** A tequila-like mezcal made in Zacatecas.

65. **Antonio Agular Mezcal**. Named after a Mexican singer.

66. **La Esclava**. No website.

67. **Real de Jalpa.** No website.

68. **Gusano Rojo**. No website.

69. **Trader Jose's Mezcal.** Found at Trader Joe's. No NOM. No distillery. What is this stuff?

70. **Mina Del Eden.** No website.

71. **San Juan Del Rio Mezcal.** No website.

The first half of the list is where all the action is for the most part. These brands are actively investing in their market presence and the category as well.

mezcalero
MEZCAL

APPENDIX 1

The Economics of Mezcal

Today, the mezcal market is tiny compared to tequila. Well, really compared to everything. According to the Distilled Spirits Council of the United States:

U.S. 2013 NINE-LITER CASE SALES

Vodka	65.9mm
Rum	25.5mm
Bourbon	18.0mm
Premium Tequila	13.1mm
Gin	10.3mm
Scotch	9.6mm
Irish Whiskey	2.5mm
Mezcal	0.1mm

The mezcal sales figure is from COMERCAM's 2013 data, and totals 93,000 nine-liter cases. With tequila sales at just over 13 million cases that means mezcal sales in the U.S. are less than 1% of tequila sales—tequila sales are approximately 140 times greater than mezcal! Stunning. On a sad note, of the 13.1 million in tequila sales, Jose Cuervo was approximately 25 percent of that. God help us all!

Let's look at Scotch, against which mezcal frequently draws comparison due to its perceived nature as an acquired, smoky taste. Scotch sales are one hundred times greater than mezcal, and even Irish whiskey is twenty six times larger. What does this mean? In my view, it means mezcal has a lot of room to run because it is every bit as good as these other categories, and actually better in my view (of course). Mezcal is a developing story—the first inning of a nine-inning game.

Mezcal has clearly made a lot of progress in recent years. We can look to tequila to see mezcal's sales potential, as I believe the premium tequila market is a great proxy for the prospects and promise of mezcal.

While mezcal statistics are very hard to come by via COMERCAM, tequila statistics, through the CRT, are readily available. The CRT (http://www.crt.org.mx/) is a great online resource to gather data on tequila sales and exports. One of the key pieces of data provided is the history of overall tequila exports plus a more granular look at premium tequila (defined as 100 percent agave) exports. In part due to the increased perception over the last ten to twenty years of tequila as a premium spirit, the export growth of the premium segment has far outpaced that of the overall tequila market. Working with the CRT export data, I find:

- In 2002, tequila exports totaled 88 million liters, 8 million of which were 100 percent agave, so 9 percent of total tequila exports came in the premium sector.
- In 2013, tequila exports totaled 172 million liters, 63 million of which were 100 percent agave, so 37 percent of total tequila exports came in the premium sector.

So over the last twelve years total tequila exports were up 95 percent, but premium tequila exports were up 600 percent! Wow. That is a compounded annual growth rate of 18 percent over twelve years. Further, the trend seems to be accelerating. Nielsen reports sales of tequilas priced $60 or higher are up 50 percent annually since 2010. As many mezcals are priced in this range, this clearly aligns well with the potential mezcal growth trend.

Many times a growth metric like that is misleading because the growth was calculated from a tiny base. But here this is not the case. Premium tequila sales were already at 8 million cases in 2002—so not tiny. Speaking of tiny, let's look at the brief history of mezcal exports:

MEZCAL EXPORTS AT 38 PERCENT ABV EQUIVALENTS (COMERCAM STATS)

Year	Total Liters	9 Liter Cases	Comments
2005	214,664	23,852	
2006	528,507	58,723	
2007	407,868	45,318	
2008	315,696	35,077	
2009	273,976	30,442	
2010	422,864	46,984	Premiums Arrive
2011	647,989	71,998	
2012	745,239	82,803	Guestimate
2013	842,489	93,609	

Mezcal exports rose quickly after certification began in 2005, but then were set back by the financial crisis. After a brief dip, mezcal sales began growing in 2010 as the economy recovered and many new premium brands began to arrive in the U.S. Since 2009, mezcal sales have increased at an annual rate of 32 percent. This is substantially higher than the growth that premium tequila has enjoyed over the past ten years. I believe mezcal will continue to see this type of growth in the coming years.

So let's have some fun with that. If mezcal were to continue growing at 32 percent a year for the next ten years, sales would be roughly 1.5 million cases in ten years. Under this scenario, there would likely be a handful of brands selling 50,000 to 100,000 cases, suggesting the large spirit companies would acquire some of these brands. The pros and cons of that were discussed in previous chapters.

For the first time in 2013, COMERCAM also provided export volumes for individual brands. Here is a selective list of brand export numbers:

Brand	9L Cases	Brand	9L Cases	Brand	9L Cases
Del Maguey Vida	10,922	La Puritita	757	Los Danzantes	318
Scorpion	4,326	Montelobos	750	Don Amado	318
Ilegal	2,598	El Zacatecano	692	Nuestro Soledad	309
Fidencio	2,597	Wild Shot	578	Agave de Cortes	257
DM Single Village	2,349	Mina Real	564	Union	217
Alipus	2,023	Alacran	383	Delirio	232
Sombra	1,920	Wahaka	370	Mezcalero	206
Pierde Almas	1,189	El Tinieblo	345	Siete Misterios	202
Peloton	1,120	El Jolgorio	333	El Silencio	158
El Buho	901	Los Nahuales	324	Tosba	116
Vago	877	Marca Negra	323	Koch	106

A few observations:

- Only nine brands sold more than 1,000 cases which is a very low hurdle. 1,000 cases is equivalent to 12,000 750ml bottles.
- I was surprised that Del Maguey's Single Village line did not have higher volumes since they have been in the market far longer than anyone else—perhaps it's due to their premium price point.
- On the other hand, Del Maguey has clearly done an excellent job placing Vida in the wells of many bars.
- I assume Peloton encompasses the broader label of Mezcales de Leyenda since Leyenda in not elsewhere on the COMERCAM list. Peloton is their cocktail version.
- I just could not bring myself to put Monte Alban and Zignum in the table, though they have respectable case numbers at 18,051 and 4,326 respectively.
- Low quality brands (yes, this is subjective) and brands with exports below 100 cases did not make the list.
- These are the total export numbers for these brands so it includes sales to any country to which they sell.

You may be embarrassed for me, but I love this kind of data! Thanks to Judah Kuper at Vago for giving me the heads up.

References

1. Alfonso A. Gardea, Lloyd T. Findley, J. Antonio Orozco-Avitia, Noemí Bañuelos, Martín Esqueda and Travis H. Huxman. "Bacanora and Sotol: So Far, So Close," *Estudios Sociales*, num. 2, marzo 2012 pp.153-168. A publication of Centro de Investigacion en Alimentacion Y Desarrollo A.C.
2. Park S. Noble, *Remarkable Agaves and Cacti* (New York: Oxford University Press, 1994), 34, 42.
3. "In Search of the Blue Agave: Mezcal", by Ian Chadwick, accessed January 2014. http://www.ianchadwick.com/tequila/mezcal.
4. Howard Scott Gentry, *Agaves of Continental North America* (The University of Arizona Press, 1982), 3-31.
5. Bob Emmons, *The Book of Tequila* (Open Court Publishing Company, 1997), 19, 25, 54, 60, 65.
6. Michael Jackson, *The Complete Guide to Single Malt Scotch* (DK Adult, 2010), 37. Reprinted from *The Complete Guide to Single Malt Scotch* by permission of DK Publishing, a division of Penguin Group (USA) LLC. Text Copyright © The Estate of Michael Jackson. Copyright © 2010 Dorling Kindersley Limited.
7. Yuri de Gortari, Edmundo Escamilla, Lisa J. Heller, *mezcal, our essence* (Ambar Diseño Publishing, 2009), 120-123.
8. "The Agave Page", The Succulent Plant Page, accessed January 2014. http://www.succulent-plant.com
9. Ted Genoways, "The Tequila Curse", *Bloomberg Business Week,* October 17, 2013. Used with permission of Bloomberg LP Copyright © 2014. All rights reserved.
10. Ana G. Valenzuela-Zapata and Gray Paul Nabhan, *¡Tequila! A Natural and Cultural History* (The University of Arizona Press, 2003), 28-29.
11. Abisai Josue Garcia Mendoza, "A Geography of Mezcal", *Artes de Mexico*, Numero 98, July 2010. 82-83.
12. Park S. Noble, Desert Wisdom / Agaves and Cacti: CO2, Water, Climate Change (iUniverse, 2010), 3-6.

GLOSSARY

Abocado – A mezcal to which flavorings, sweeteners, colorings or other additives have been added.

Aguamiel – Translated as "honey water." This is the liquid taken from certain species of mature agave which can then be fermented into pulque.

Alembic – An old-fashioned copper or "pot still" believed to be introduced to Mexico by the Spanish.

Autoclave – A large industrial oven/pressure cooker typically used in tequila production. Autoclaves cook the agaves much faster than ovens and many feel the resulting tequila suffers as a result.

Bagaso – The agave fibers after roasting and crushing.

Coa – A flat, sharp, half-moon-shaped blade attached to a long wooden stick which is used by the cortador to cut the agave leaves down to the base of the piña.

Colas – Translated as the "tails," or last of the alcohol that comes out of the distillation and is quite bitter in taste.

COMERCAM – Common acronym for the agency that regulates mezcal production and certification in Mexico.

Corazon – Translated as "heart," and this is the center or sweet spot of the distillation which contains the most desirable alcohol.

Cortador – The harvester of the agave plant who trims the leaves and uproots the piña at maturity

CRT – Common acronym for the agency that regulates tequila production and certification in Mexico.

Horno – Translated as "oven," this is the traditional earthen pit used for cooking the agave piñas in mezcal production.

Jimador – In the tequila world, this is the term used for the cortador

Las Perlas – Translated as "the pearls," the bubbles that form on the surface of a distillate when shaken or vigorously streamed into a container. Mezcaleros can accurately deduce the ABV of the mezcal by observing las perlas.

Maguey – Common term for the agave plant in Mexico.

Master Mezcalero – One who has achieved recognition from his peers as an outstanding mezcal producer.

Mayahuel – The Aztec goddess of fertility and the maguey plant.

Mezcalero – One who makes mezcal.

NOM – Norma Oficial Mexicana. A unique number assigned to each certified mezcal producer.

Norma – The law that governs the production, bottling, etc. of a specific product in Mexico. Mezcal is governed by "NOM-070-SCFI-1994."

Palenque – I liken a palenque to a farm throughout the book, though admittedly that descriptor does not quite capture it. These are very small distilleries with little technology and a very rustic appearance—perhaps a farm, but with no animals.

Pechuga – Translated as "breast," a pechuga describes a mezcal that has been distilled twice and then is redistilled a third time by loading wild and seasonal fruits and nuts into the still while suspending a raw, clean, skinned chicken breast (most typically) within the still so the vapors pass over and through it before condensing back to alcohol. Pechugas can be made with chicken, turkey, rabbit, deer meat or other proteins, and sometimes no protein at all.

Penca – The succulent leave of an agave plant.

Piña – The heart of the agave plant which contains the starches necessary for mezcal production.

Puntas – Translated as the "head," or first alcohol that comes off the distillation which contains undesirable smells, flavors and chemicals.

Tahona – A large stone wheel pulled by a horse, mule or tractor which is used to crush the agave fibers after they have been roasted.

Tepache – The fermented bagaso mash which is loaded into the still for distillation.

ACKNOWLEDGMENTS AND PHOTO CREDITS

There are many people to thank for their assistance in putting this book together. First, my wife Maria—my Mezcal Muse—for her encouragement and incredible patience as this book became an all-consuming project. And of course, our enthusiastic son Nico who knows more about mezcal than any ten-year-old should! My close friend and agave conspirator Mario Yrun for his tireless and meticulous editing skills, not to mention his superlative mezcal palate. My parents, Marilyn McEvoy and Bill Kennedy, for their positive energy and thoughtful comments on how to strengthen the book.

Fred Antonacci, thank you for your early comments on the manuscript and quick turnaround. Raza Zaidi, for your pointed remarks and amusing sidebars. Steve Myers, I appreciate your mezcal insights and skilled turn of phrase. John Rexer, for your zeal and additions to the sustainability chapter. Steve Olson for your views on how agave varieties influence the taste of mezcal and his ongoing mezcal mentorship. Eric Bigelsen from Agave Idiots, for your tequila perspective plus the "cactus" bottle! Dave Ivey for your tremendous editing skills and pointed attention to every detail in the book.

Patricia Fabricant, the incomparable book designer, thanks for putting up with my endless series of "just a few more tweaks", and doing such a stunning job designing and laying-out the entire book.

Noah Fecks, professional photographer to the stars of the spirits and culinary world, thank you for working miles beneath your pay grade with great passion and transcendent karma—the amazing cocktail and bottle shots you see in this book are his! And thanks to his outstanding assistant Greta Titelman and mixologist Sophia Urista.

Kaj Hackinen, Back Bay Importers (importer of El Jolgorio Mezcal), for access to your photo library. Raza Zaidi and the team at Wahaka Mezcal for allowing me to raid their multiple thousands of photos. John Rexer for access to the Ilegal library of palenques, production and agave shots. Gustavo Estrada at Ilegal Mezcal for being so helpful and accommodating my "emergency picture requests". Steve Olson and Ron Cooper of Del Maguey for providing fantastic mezcal production and agave shots. And finally, thank you to Mannie LaSalle of the fabulous Los Americanos restaurant in Tribeca for allowing two photo shoots at her restaurant—what a place you have!

6768758R00114

Printed in Great Britain
by Amazon.co.uk, Ltd.,
Marston Gate.